FOR ORGANS, PIANOS & ELECTRONIC KEYBOARDS

E-Z PLAY TODAY

158

LENNON LEGEND
The very best of John Lennon

ISBN 978-0-7935-2559-1

HAL•LEONARD®
7777 W. BLUEMOUND RD. P.O. BOX 13819 MILWAUKEE, WI 53213

Visit Hal Leonard Online at
www.halleonard.com

Beautiful Boy
(Darling Boy)

Registration 2
Rhythm: Rock or Jazz Rock

Words and Music by
John Lennon

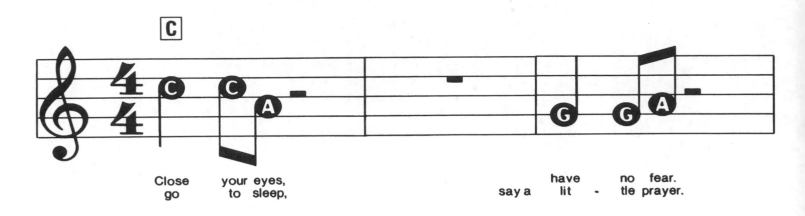

Close your eyes,
go to sleep,
say a lit - tle prayer.
have no fear.

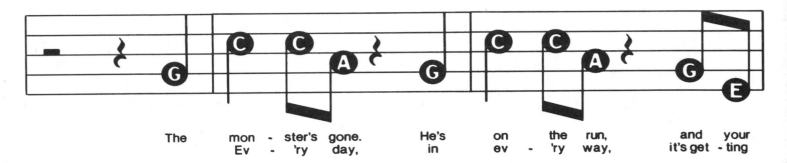

The mon - ster's gone. He's on the run, and your
Ev - 'ry day, in ev - 'ry way, it's get - ting

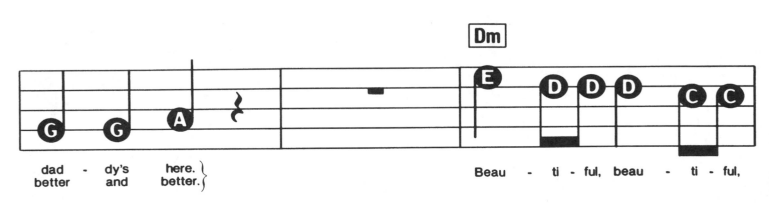

dad - dy's here.
better and better.

Beau - ti - ful, beau - ti - ful,

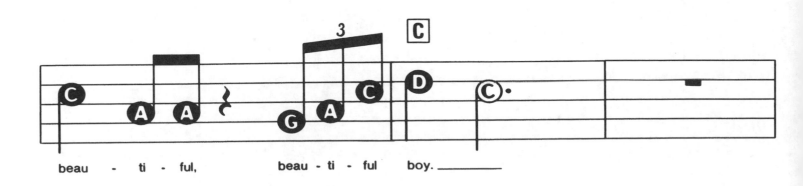

beau - ti - ful, beau - ti - ful boy. _____

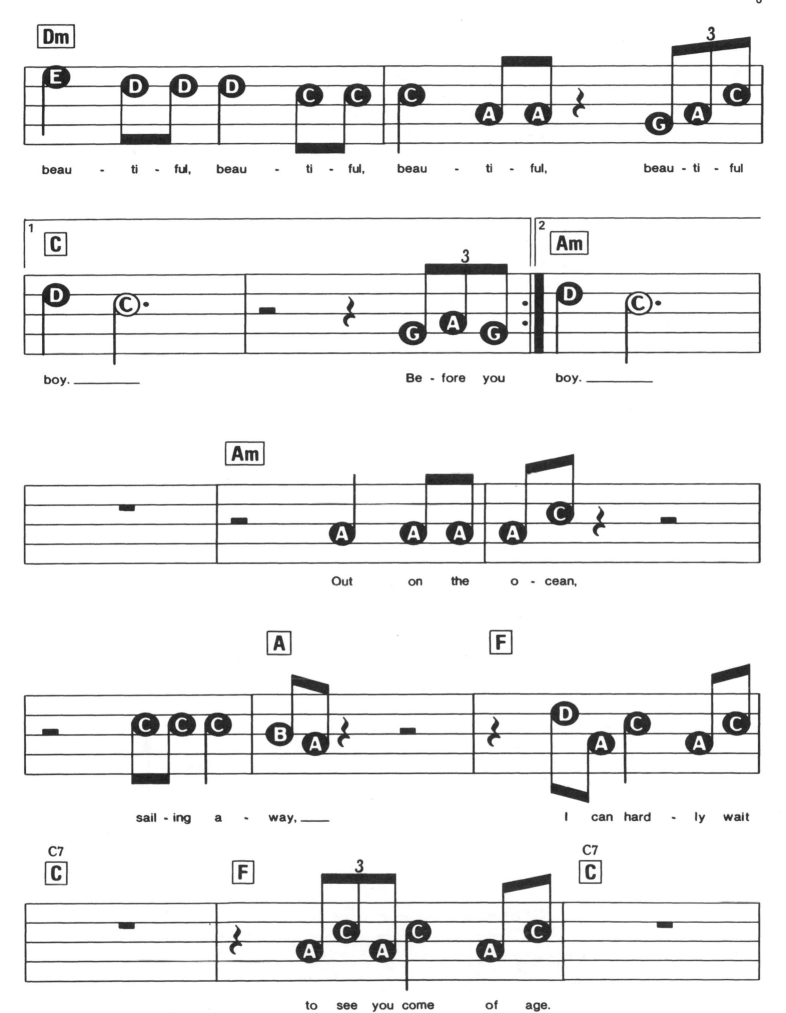

But I guess we'll both just have to be pa - tient.

'Cause it's a long _____ way to go,

a hard row to hoe. Yes, it's a

long _____ way to go, but in the mean - time,

be - fore you cross the street,

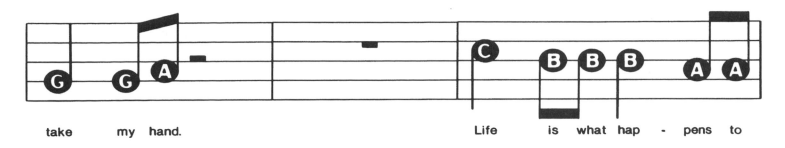

take my hand.   Life is what hap - pens to

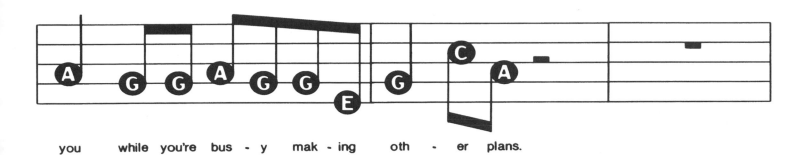

you while you're bus - y mak - ing oth - er plans.

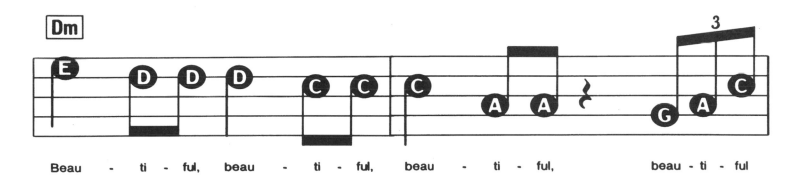

Beau - ti - ful, beau - ti - ful, beau - ti - ful, beau - ti - ful

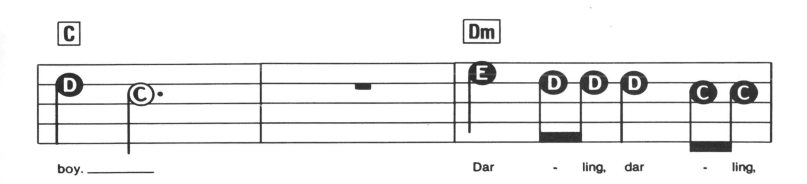

boy. _____   Dar - ling, dar - ling,

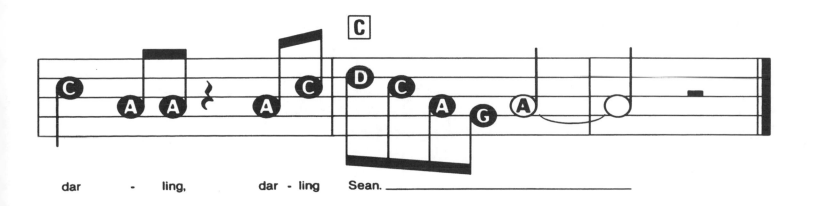

dar - ling, dar - ling Sean. _____

Borrowed Time

Registration 4
Rhythm: Calypso or Rock

Words and Music by
John Lennon

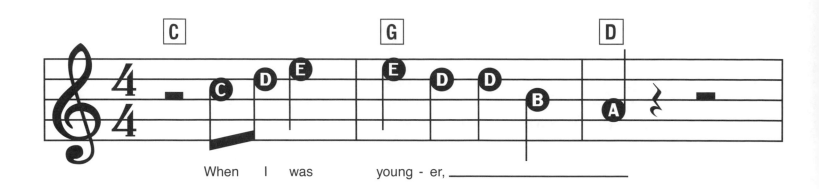

When I was young - er, _____

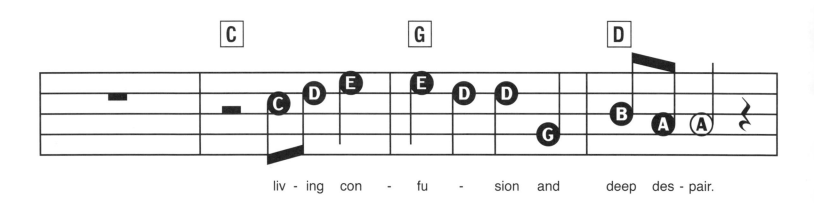

liv - ing con - fu - sion and deep des - pair.

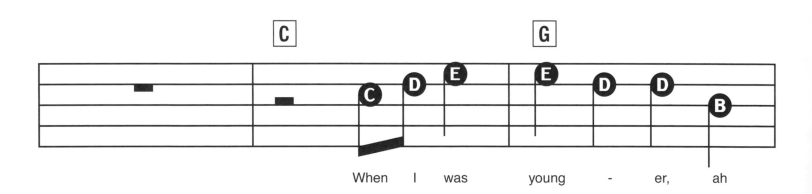

When I was young - er, ah

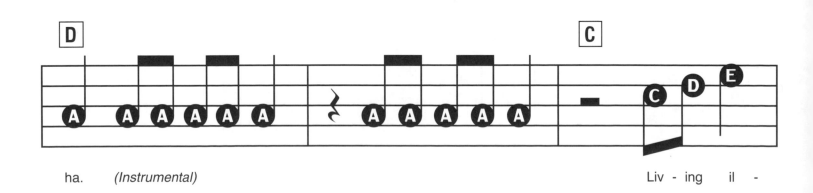

ha. *(Instrumental)*

Liv - ing il -

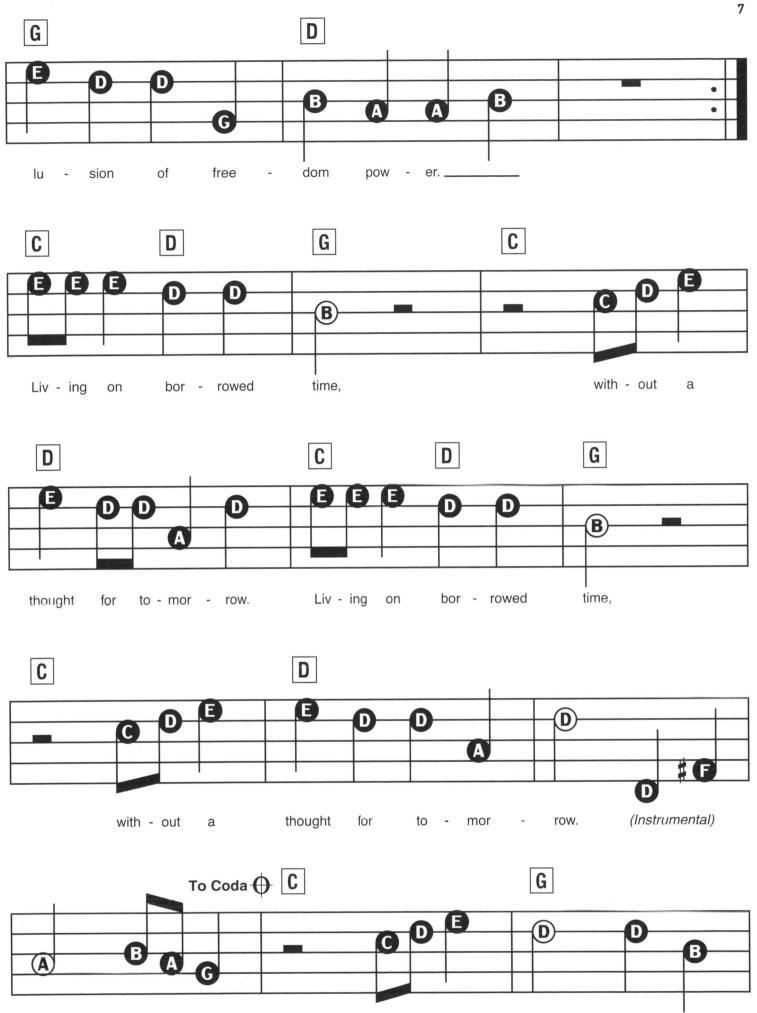

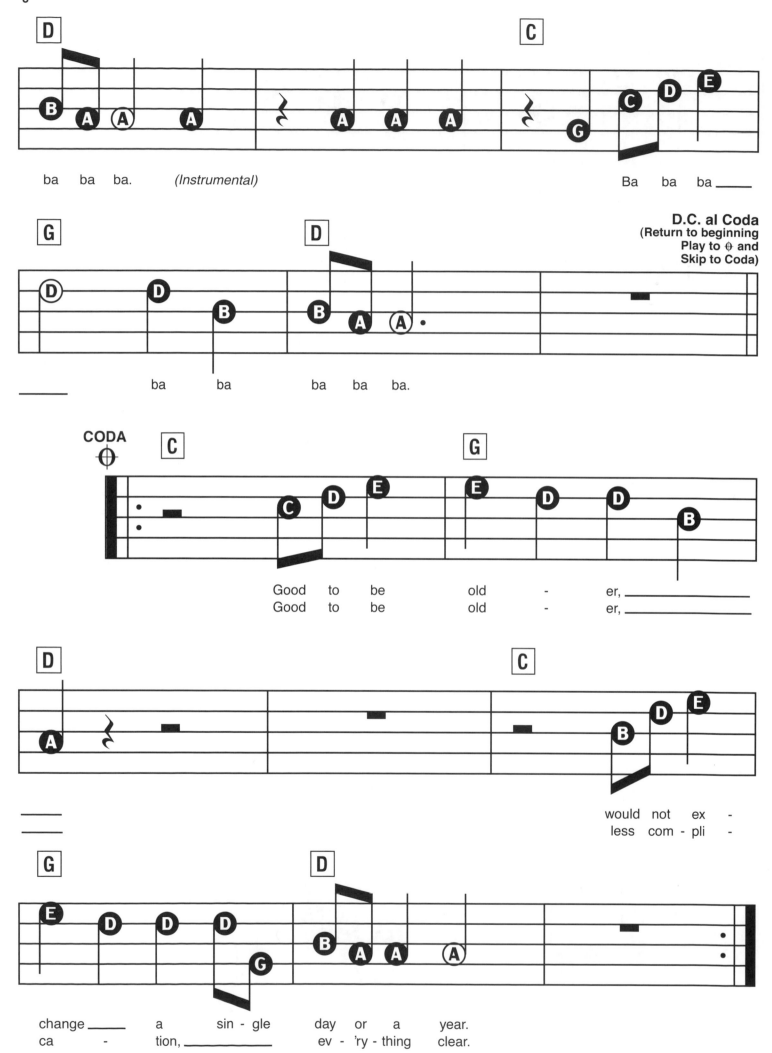

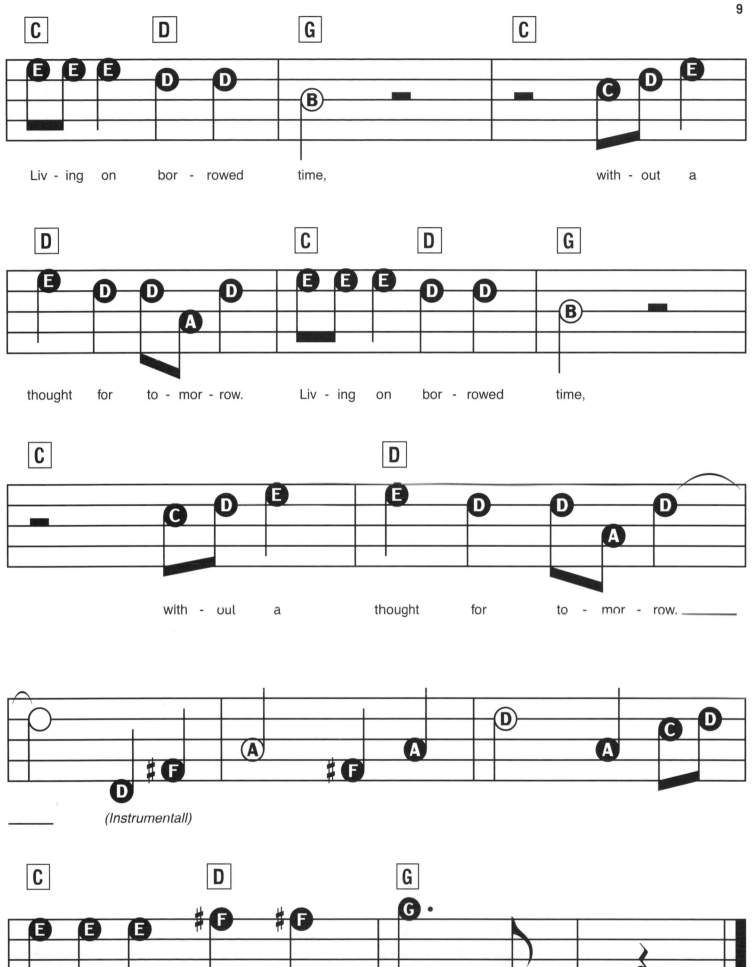

Liv - ing on bor - rowed time, with - out a

thought for to - mor - row. Liv - ing on bor - rowed time,

with - out a thought for to - mor - row. _____

_____ (Instrumentall)

Cold Turkey

Registration 4
Rhythm: Rock

Words and Music by
John Lennon

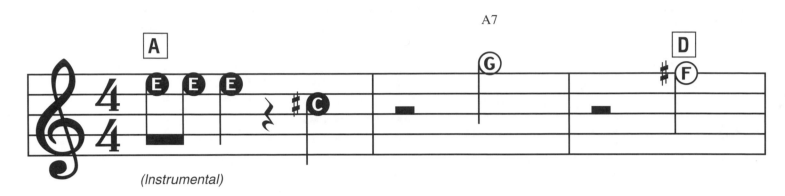

(Instrumental)

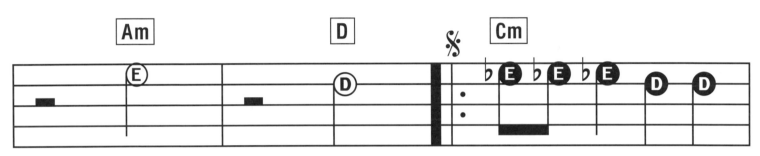

Tem - p'ra - ture's ris - ing,
bod - y is ach - ing,
Thir - ty - six hours, _____

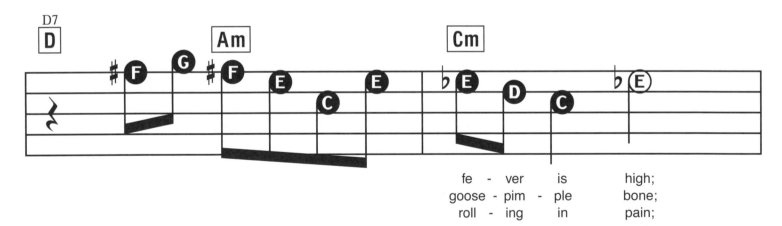

fe - ver is high;
goose - pim - ple bone;
roll - ing in pain;

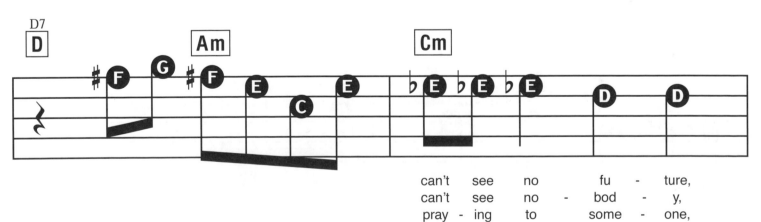

can't see no fu - ture,
can't see no - bod - y,
pray - ing to some - one,

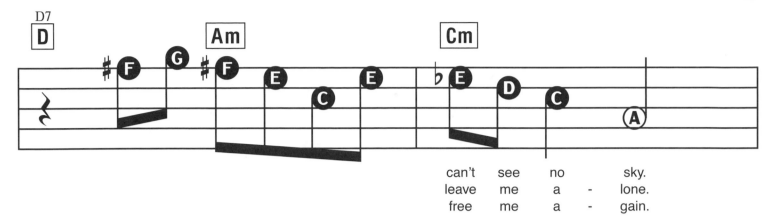

can't see no sky.
leave me a - lone.
free me a - gain.

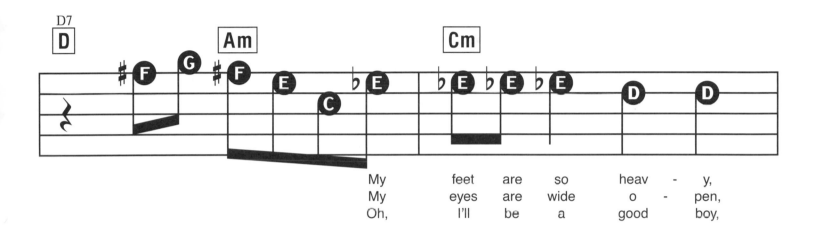

My feet are so heav - y,
My eyes are so wide o - pen,
Oh, I'll be a good boy,

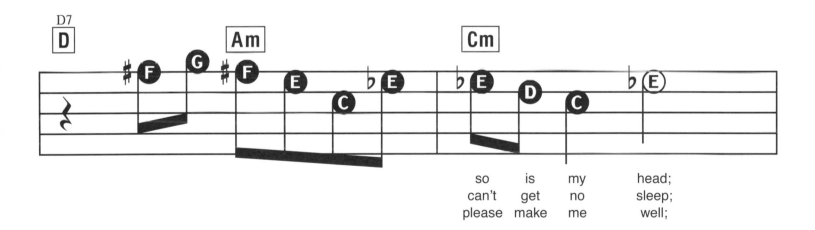

so is my head;
can't get no sleep;
please make me well;

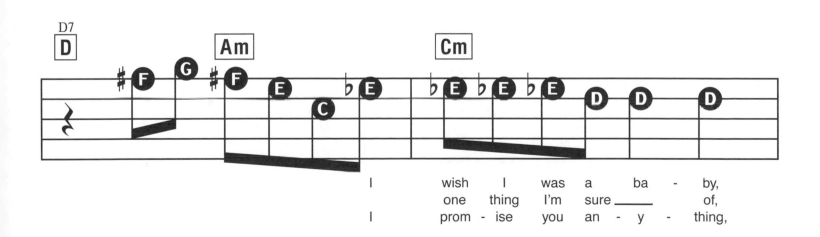

I wish I was a ba - by,
one thing I'm sure ____ of,
I prom - ise you an - y - thing,

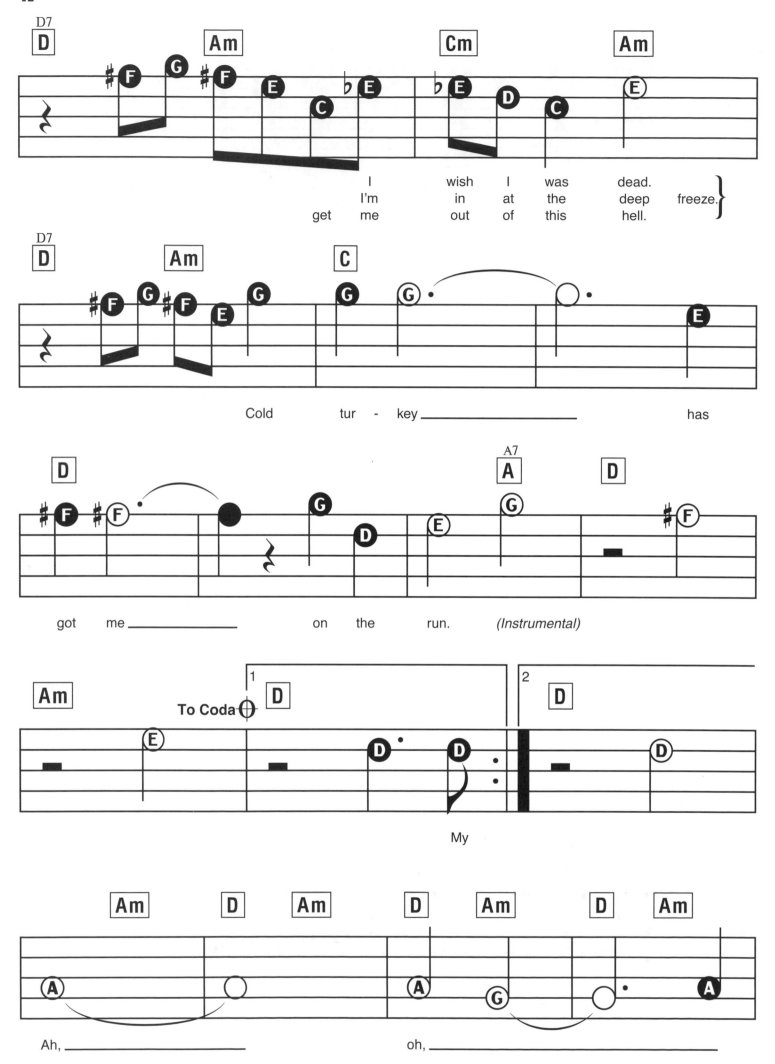

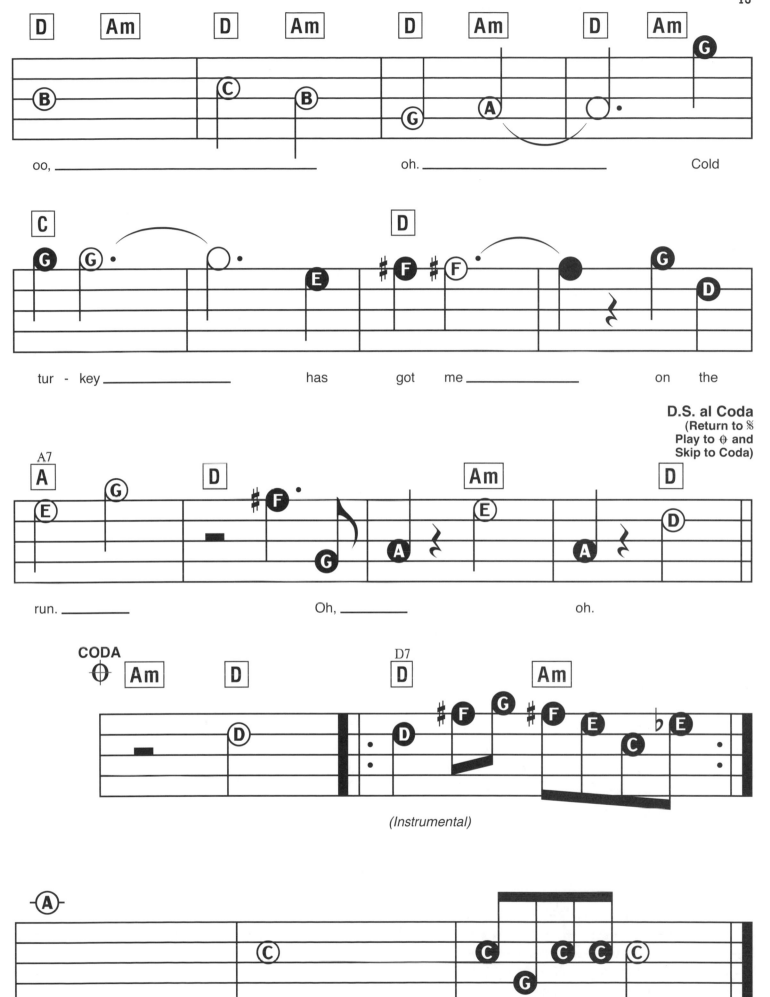

oo, _____ oh. _____ Cold

tur - key _____ has got me _____ on the

D.S. al Coda
(Return to 𝄋
Play to ⊕ and
Skip to Coda)

run. _____ Oh, _____ oh.

CODA

(Instrumental)

Give Peace a Chance

Registration 5
Rhythm: Rock or Jazz Rock

Words and Music by
John Lennon

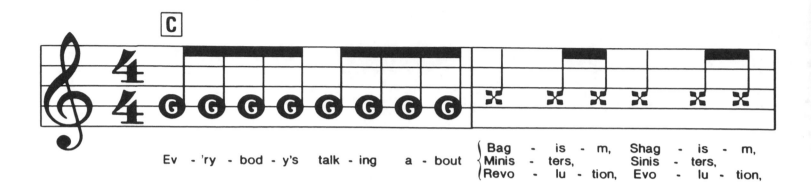

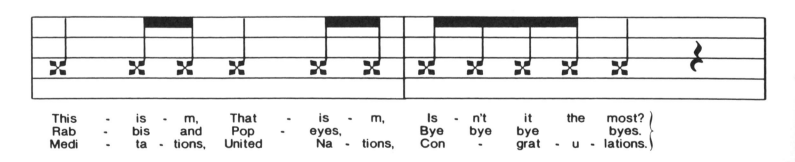

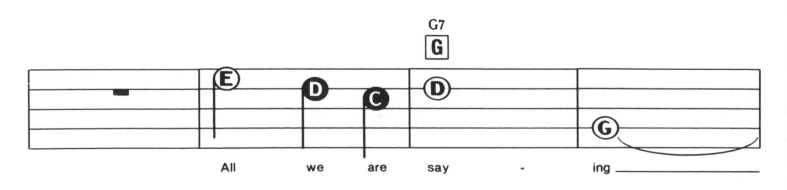

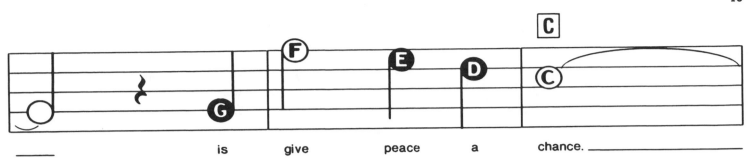

is give peace a chance. _____

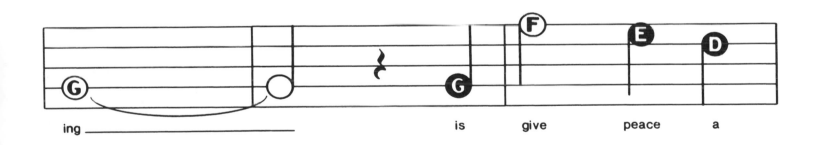

All we are say-

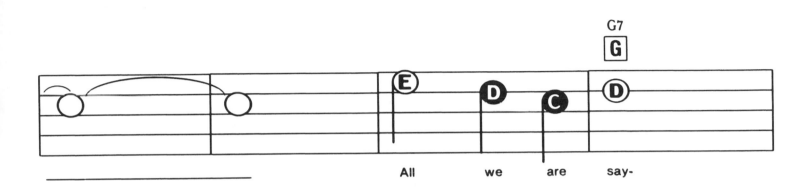

ing _____ is give peace a

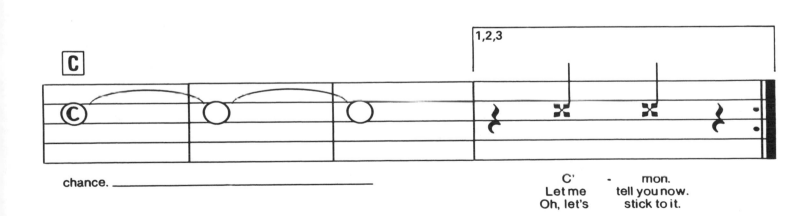

chance. _____

C' - mon.
Let me tell you now.
Oh, let's stick to it.

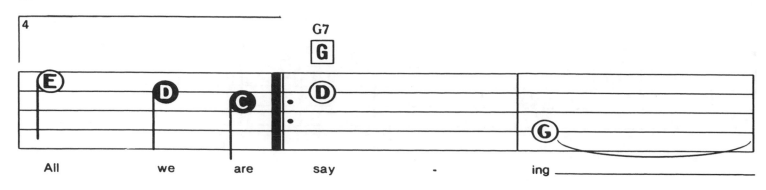

All   we   are   say - ing _____

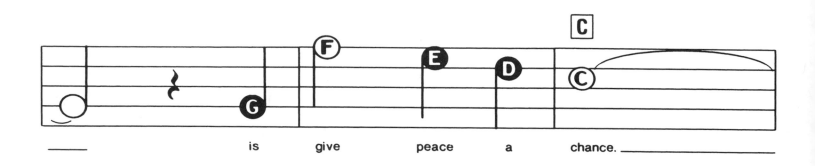

_____   is   give   peace   a   chance. _____

_____   All   we   are

4. Ev'rybody's talking about
   John and Yoko, Timmy Leary, Rosemary, Tommy Smothers,
   Bobby Dylan, Tommy Cooper, Derek Taylor, Norman Mailer,
   Alan Ginsberg, Hare Krishna, Hare, Hare Krishna
   (Repeat Refrain)

Happy Xmas
(War Is Over)

Registration 1
Rhythm: Slow Rock

Words and Music by John Lennon
and Yoko Ono

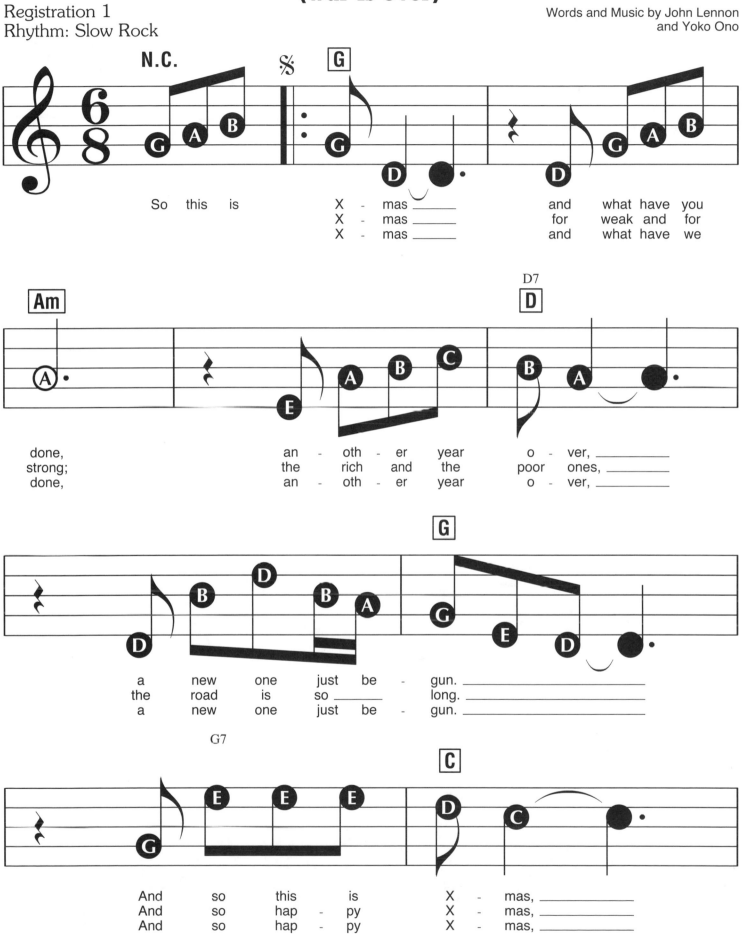

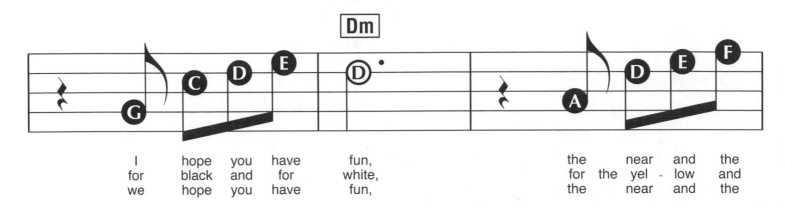

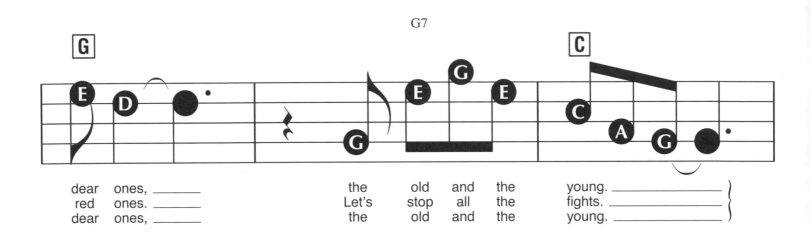

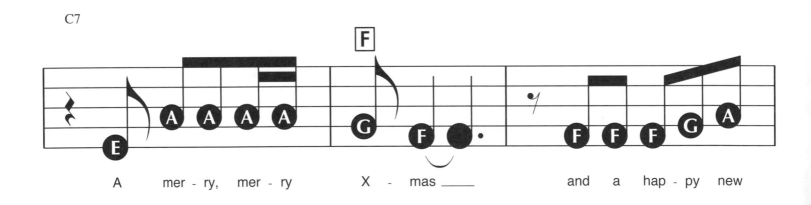

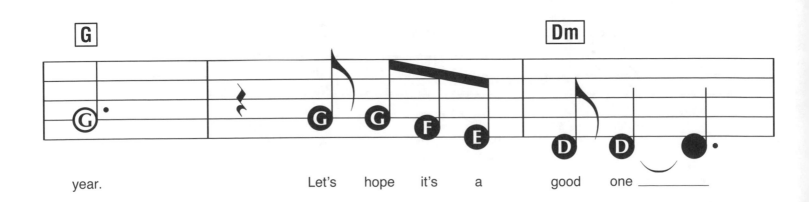

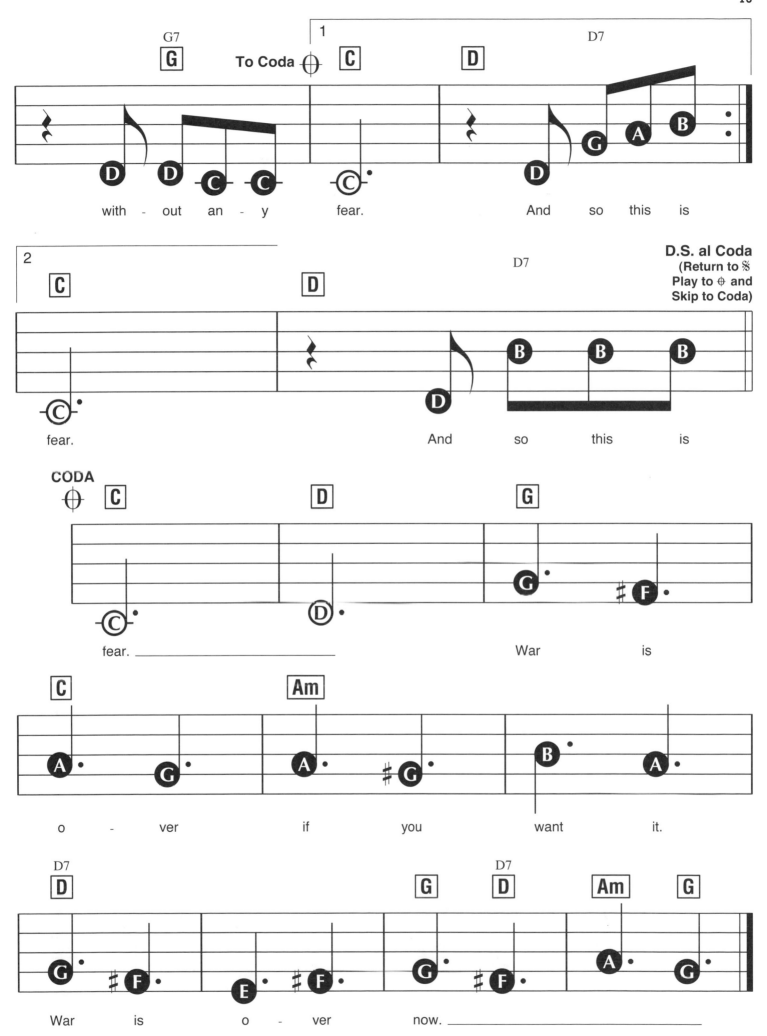

Imagine

Registration 8
Rhythm: Ballad

Words and Music by
John Lennon

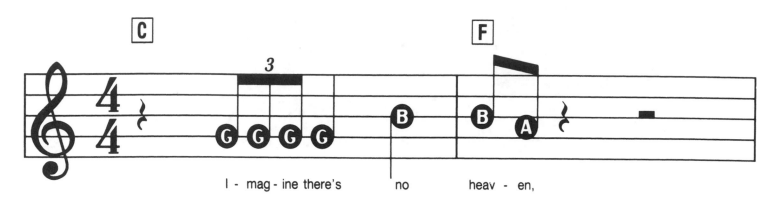

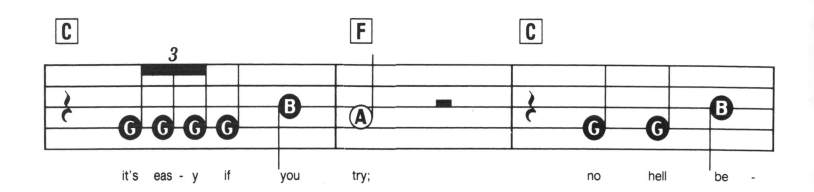

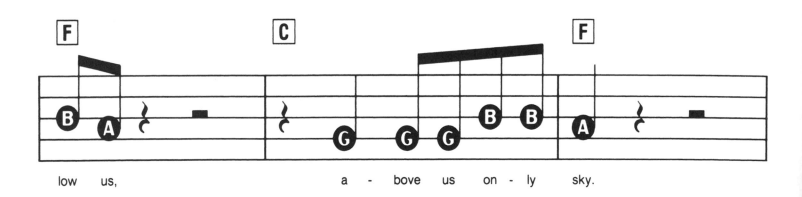

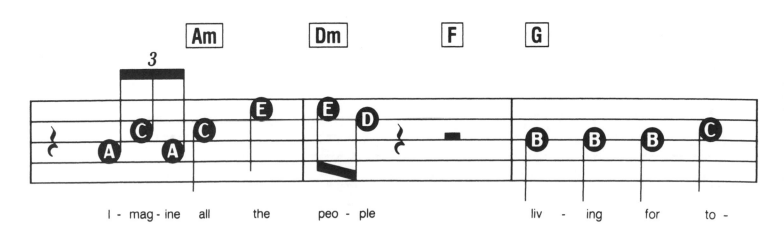

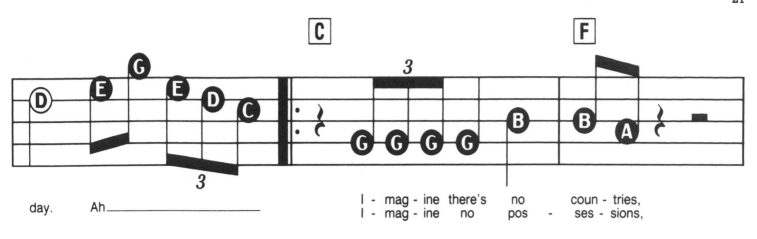

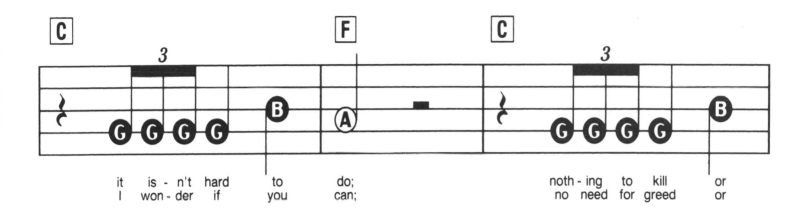

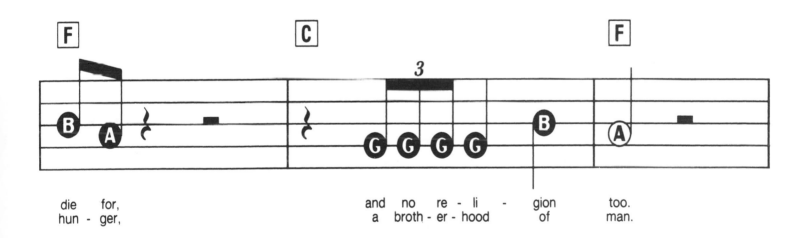

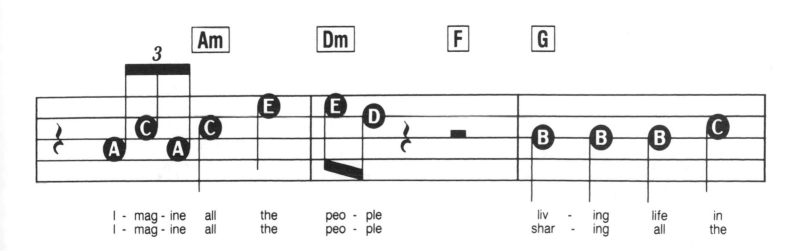

22

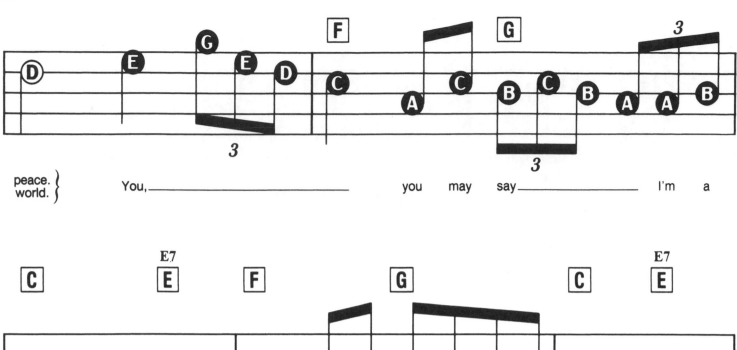

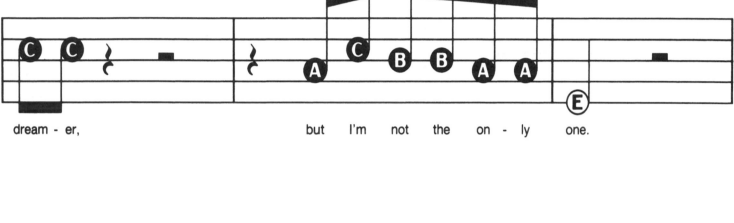

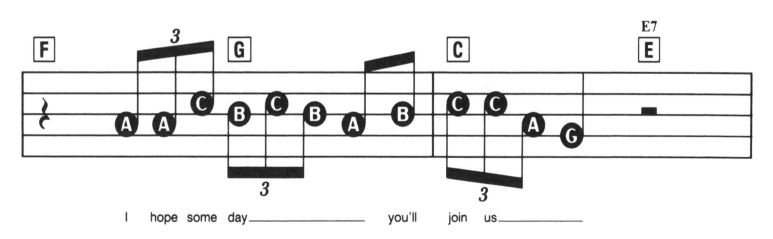

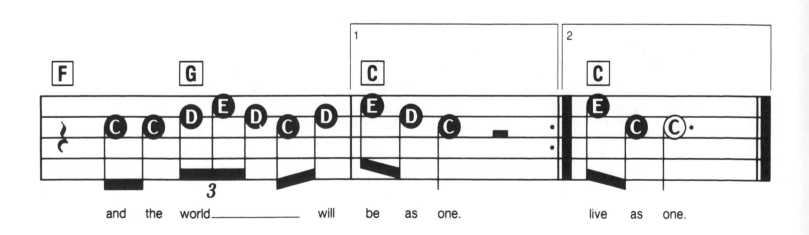

Instant Karma

Registration 3
Rhythm: Slow Rock or Swing

Words and Music by
John Lennon

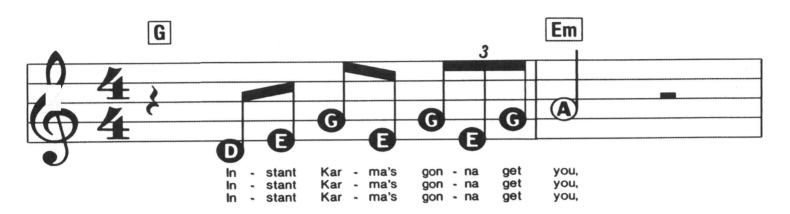

In - stant Kar - ma's gon - na get you,
In - stant Kar - ma's gon - na get you,
In - stant Kar - ma's gon - na get you,

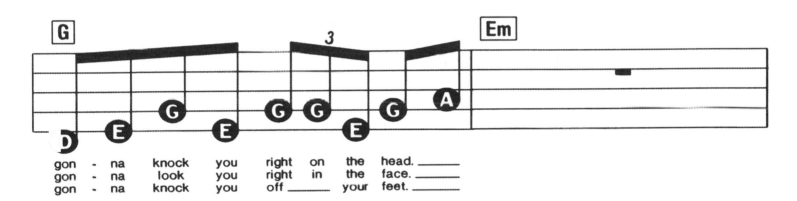

gon - na knock you right on the head.
gon - na look you right in the face.
gon - na knock you off your feet.

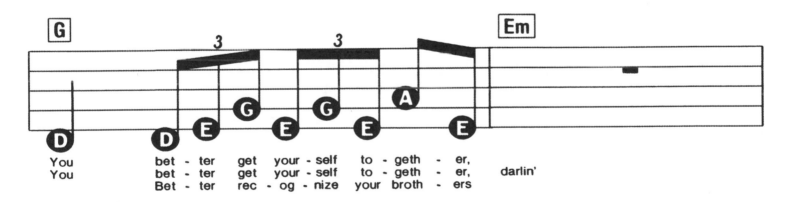

You bet - ter get your - self to - geth - er,
You bet - ter get your - self to - geth - er, darlin'
Bet - ter rec - og - nize your broth - ers

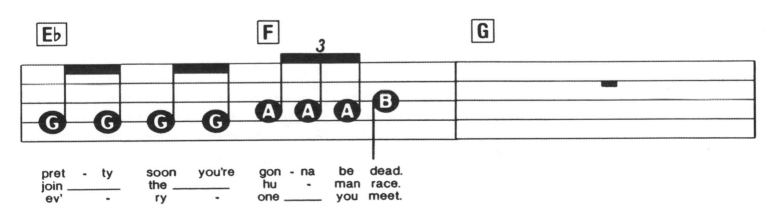

pret - ty soon you're gon - na be dead.
join the hu - man race.
ev' - ry - one you meet.

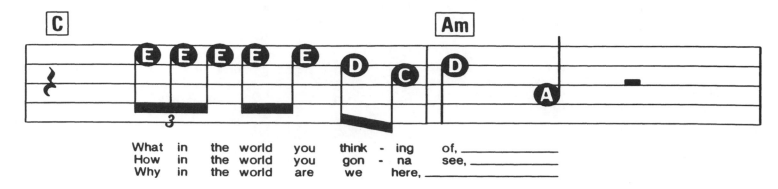

What in the world you think - ing of, _____
How in the world you gon - na see, _____
Why in the world are we here, _____

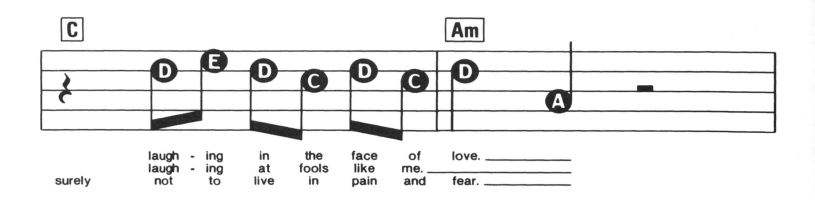

laugh - ing in the face of love. _____
laugh - ing at fools like me. _____
surely not to live in pain and fear. _____

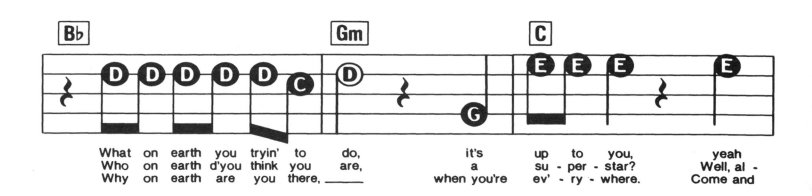

What on earth you tryin' to do, it's up to you, yeah
Who on earth d'you think you are, a su - per - star? Well, al -
Why on earth are you there, _____ when you're ev' - ry - where. Come and

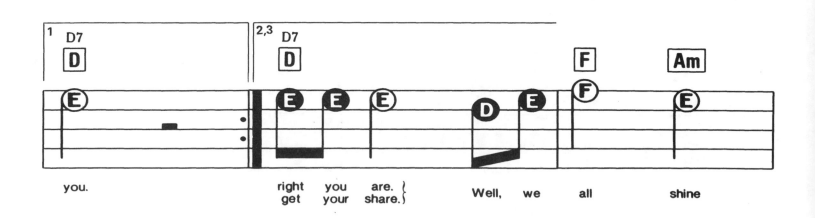

you.
right you are. } Well, we all shine
get your share.

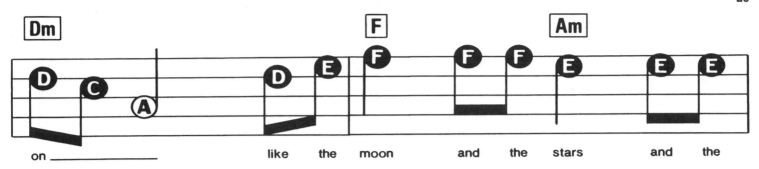

on _____ like the moon and the stars and the

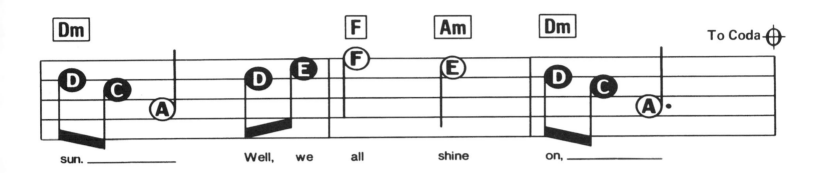

sun. _____ Well, we all shine on, _____

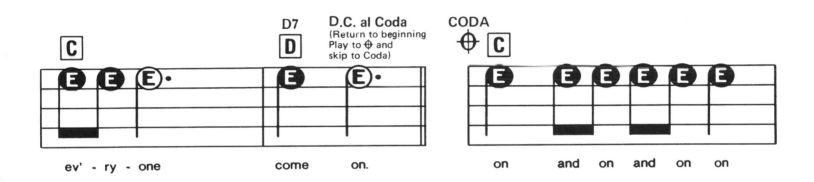

ev' - ry - one come on.

on and on and on on

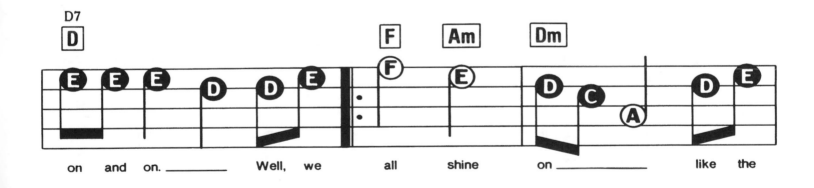

on and on. _____ Well, we all shine on _____ like the

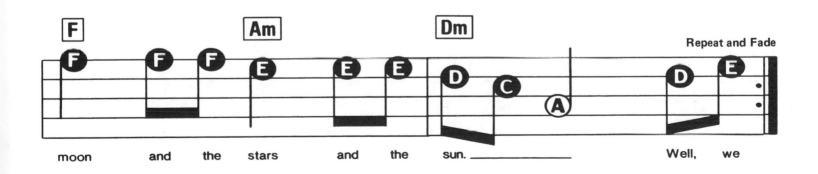

moon and the stars and the sun. _____ Well, we

Jealous Guy

Registration 4
Rhythm: Rock or Jazz Rock

Words and Music by
John Lennon

Love

Registration 8
Rhythm: Rock or Slow Rock

Words and Music by
John Lennon

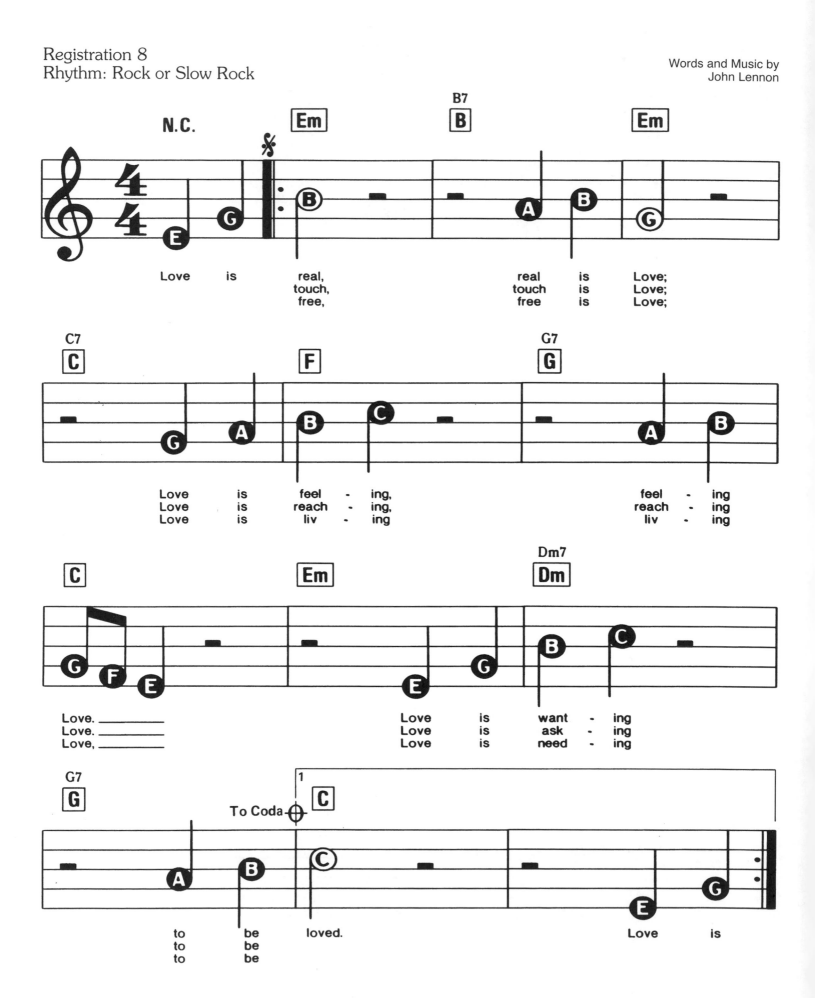

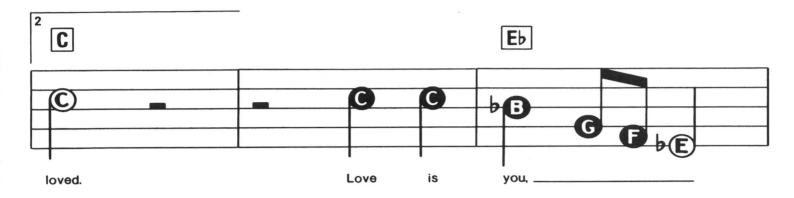

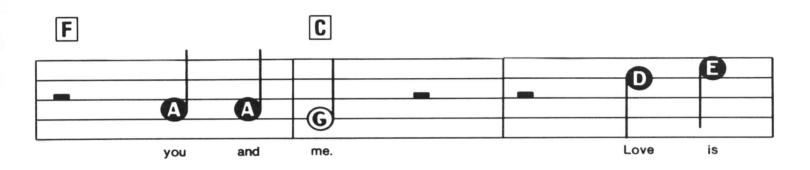

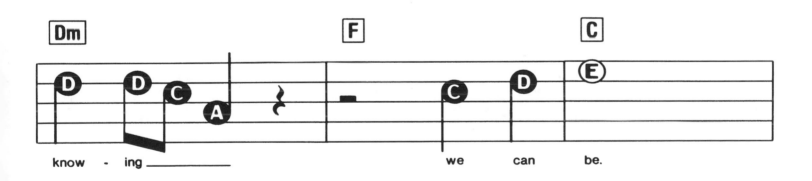

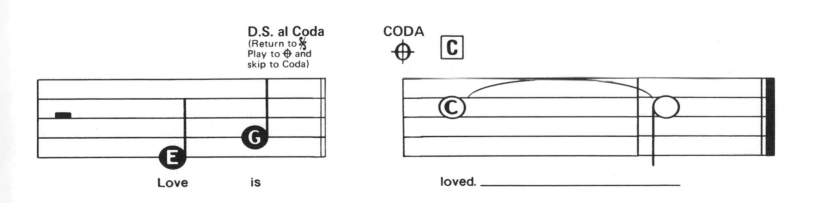

Mind Games

Registration 5
Rhythm: Rock or Slow Rock

Words and Music by
John Lennon

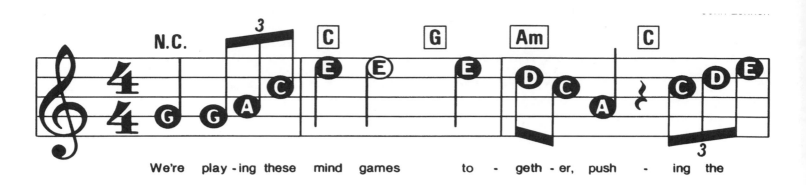

We're play-ing these mind games to - geth - er, push - ing the

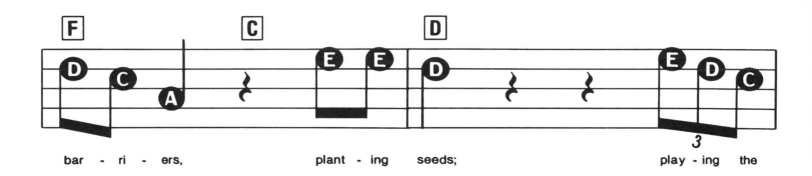

bar - ri - ers, plant - ing seeds; play - ing the

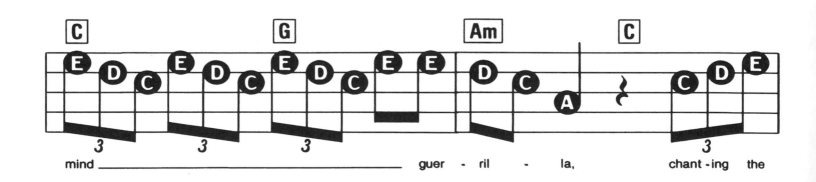

mind _____ guer - ril - la, chant - ing the

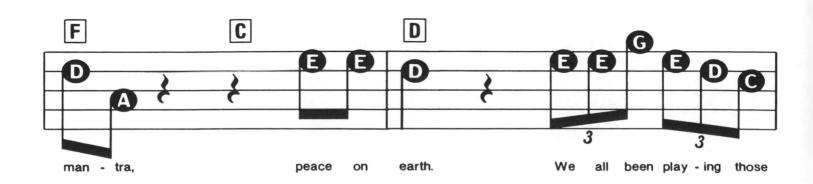

man - tra, peace on earth. We all been play - ing those

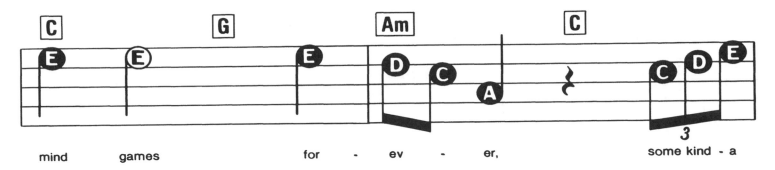

mind   games   for - ev - er,   some kind - a

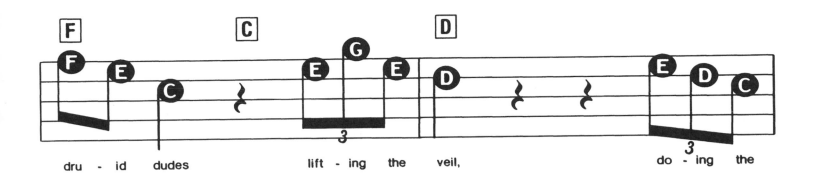

dru - id   dudes   lift - ing   the   veil,   doing   the

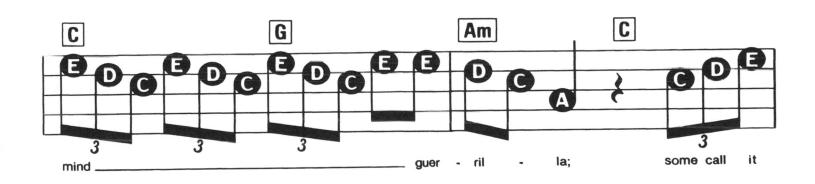

mind _____ guer - ril - la;   some call   it

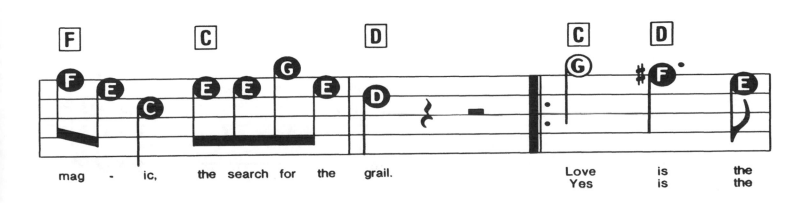

mag - ic,   the   search   for   the   grail.   Love   is   the
                                                       Yes   is   the

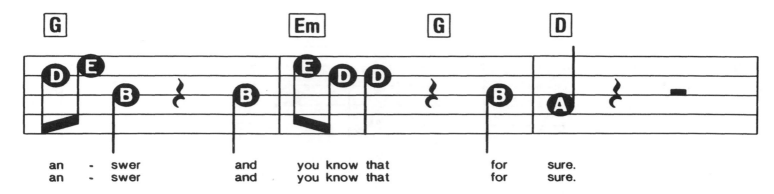

an - swer   and   you know that   for   sure.
an - swer   and   you know that   for   sure.

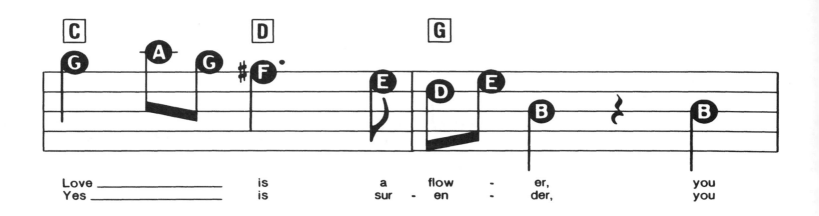

Love _____ is   a   flow - er,   you
Yes _____ is   sur - en - der,   you

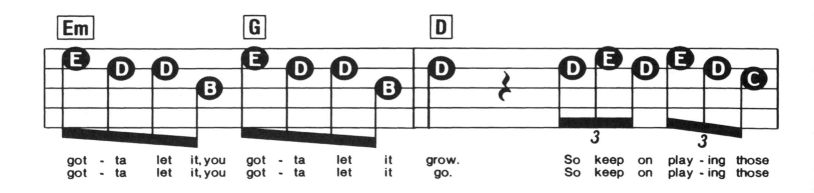

got - ta   let it, you   got - ta   let it   grow.   So keep on play - ing those
got - ta   let it, you   got - ta   let it   go.   So keep on play - ing those

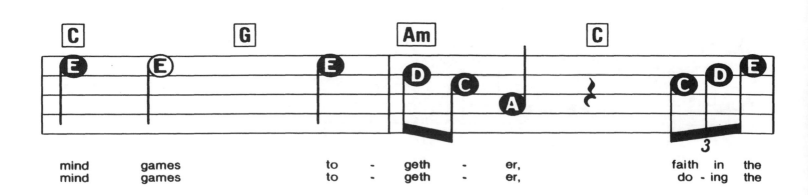

mind   games   to - geth - er,   faith in the
mind   games   to - geth - er,   do - ing the

33

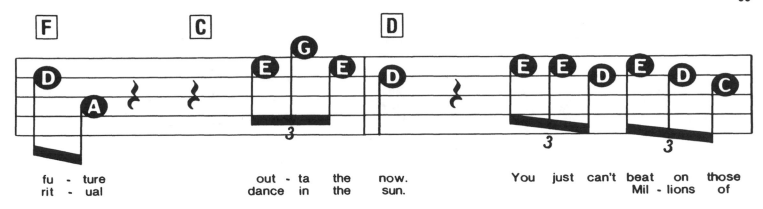

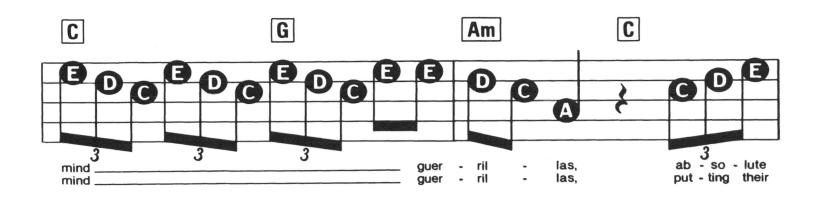

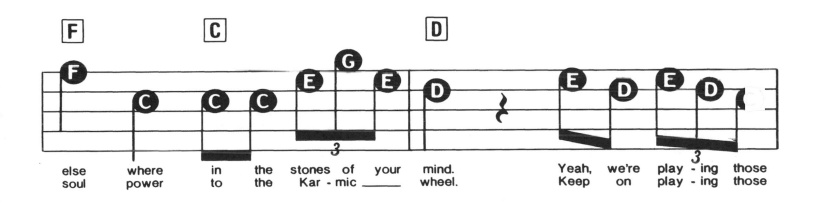

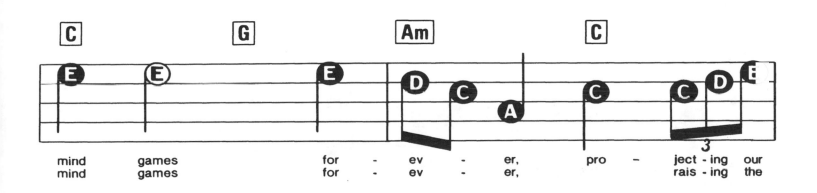

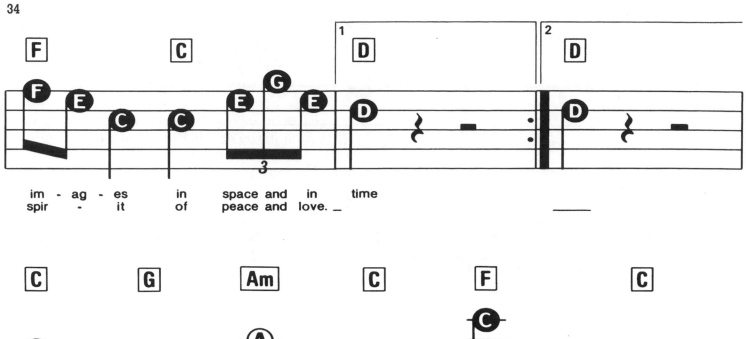

im - ag - es   in   space and   in   time
spir - it   of   peace and love. _   _____

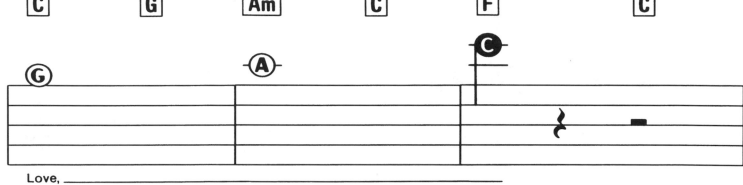

Love, _____

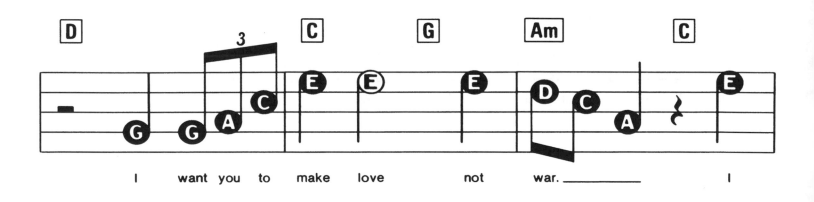

I   want you   to   make   love   not   war. _____   I

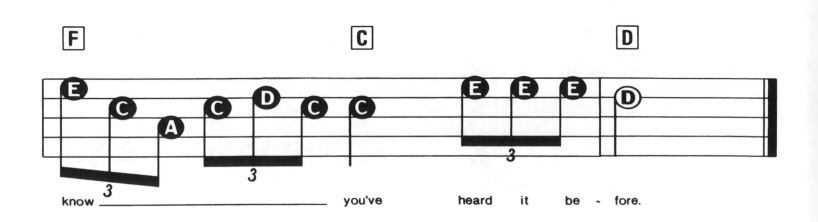

know _____ you've   heard   it   be - fore.

#9 Dream

Registration 1
Rhythm: Slow Rock or Ballad

Words and Music by
John Lennon

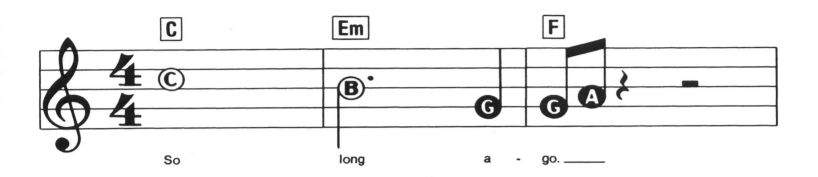

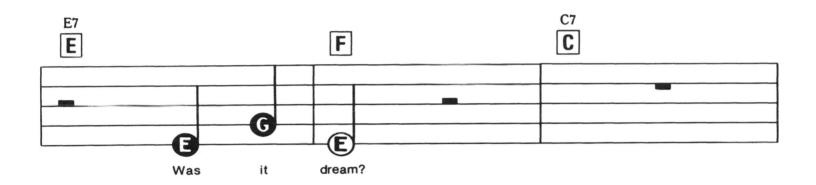

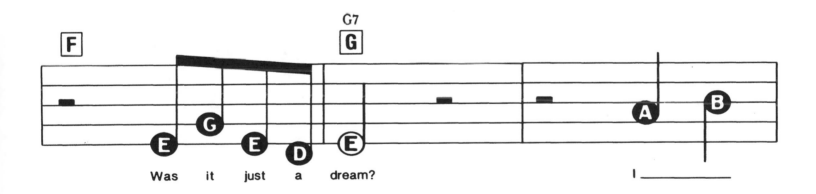

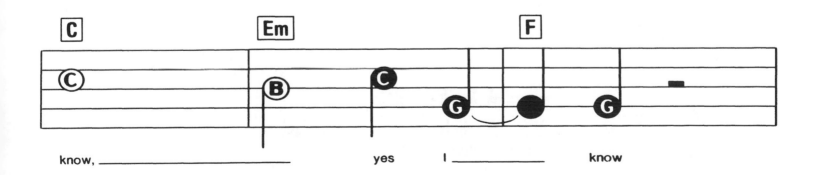

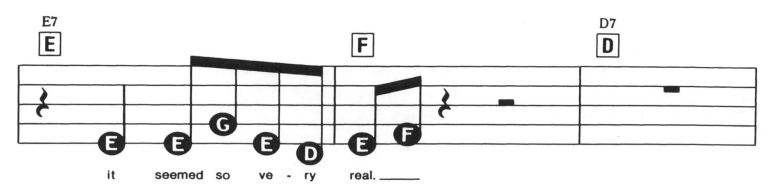

it seemed so ve - ry real. _____

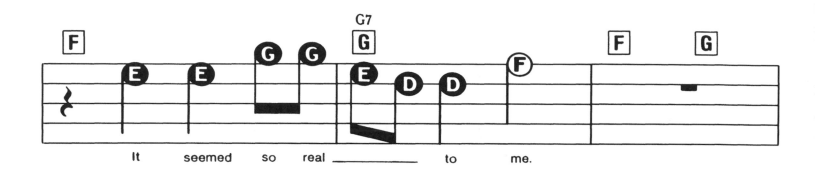

It seemed so real _____ to me.

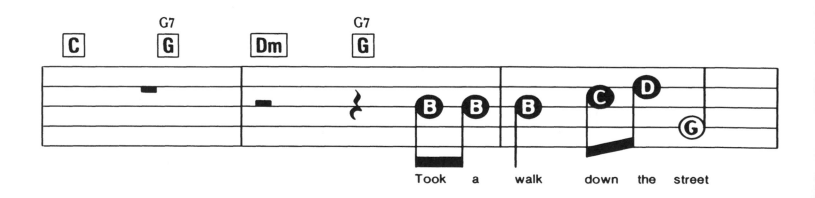

Took a walk down the street

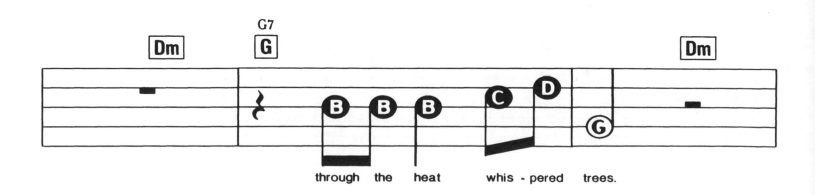

through the heat whis - pered trees.

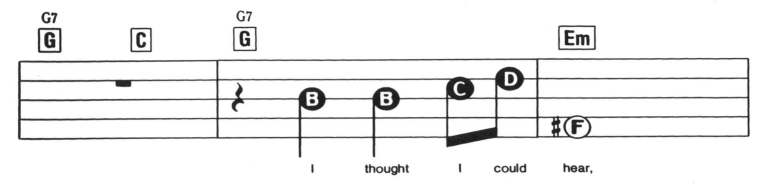

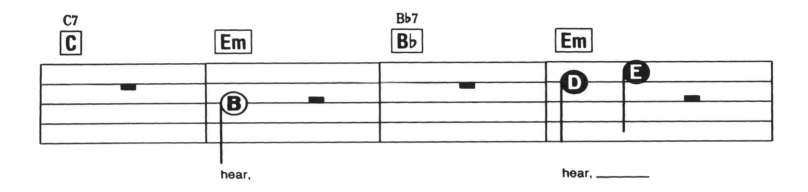

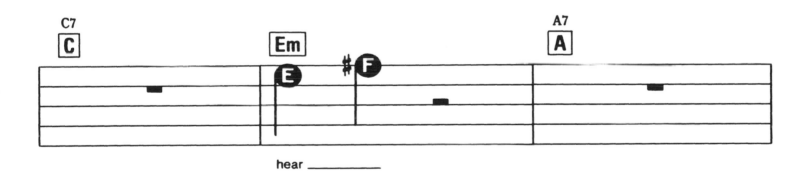

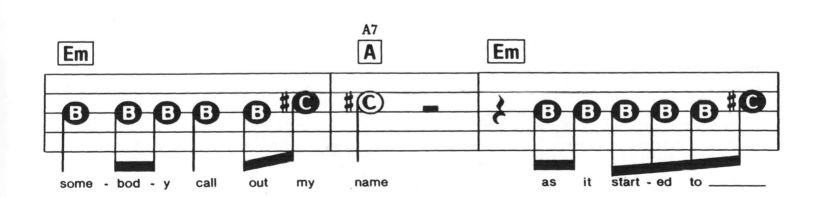

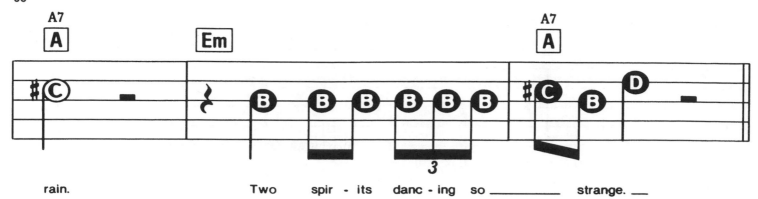

rain.　　　　　　　　Two　spir - its　danc - ing　so _____ strange. __

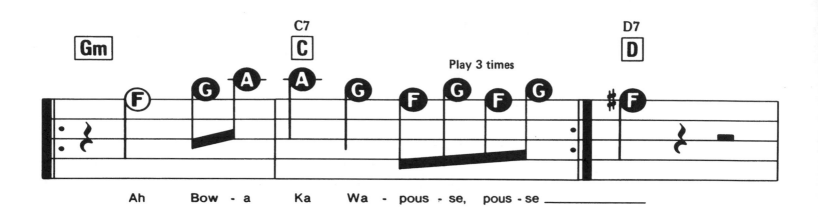

Ah　Bow - a　Ka　Wa - pous - se,　pous - se _____

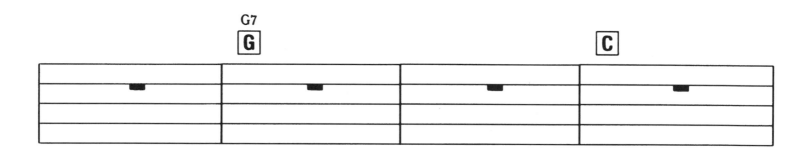

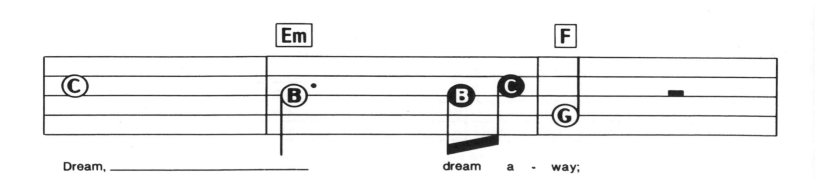

Dream, _____　　dream　a - way;

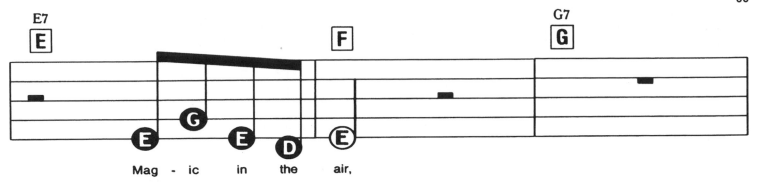

Mag - ic in the air,

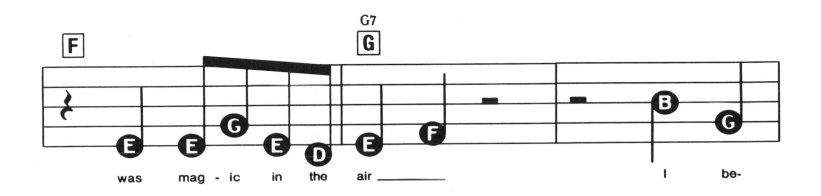

was mag - ic in the air _____ I be-

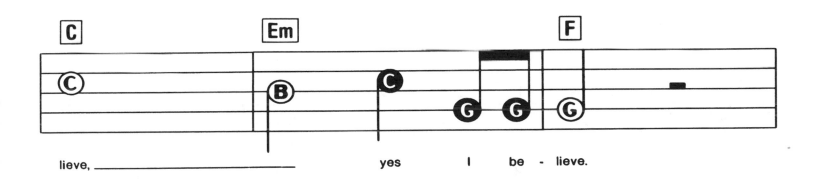

lieve, _____ yes I be - lieve.

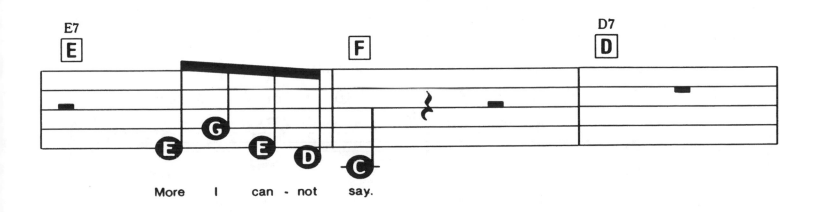

More I can - not say.

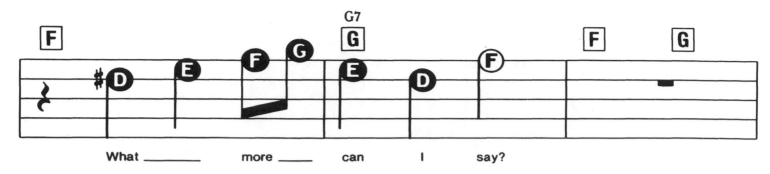

What _____ more _____ can I say?

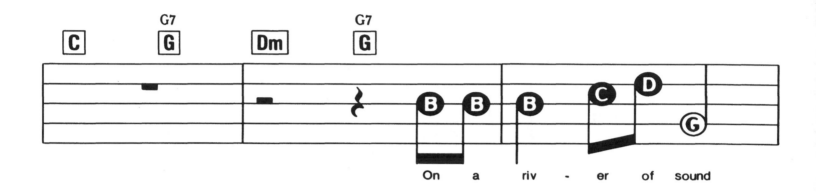

On a riv - er of sound

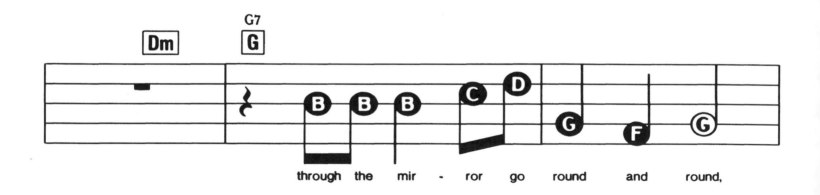

through the mir - ror go round and round,

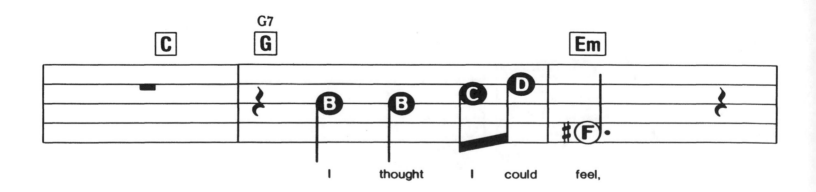

I thought I could feel,

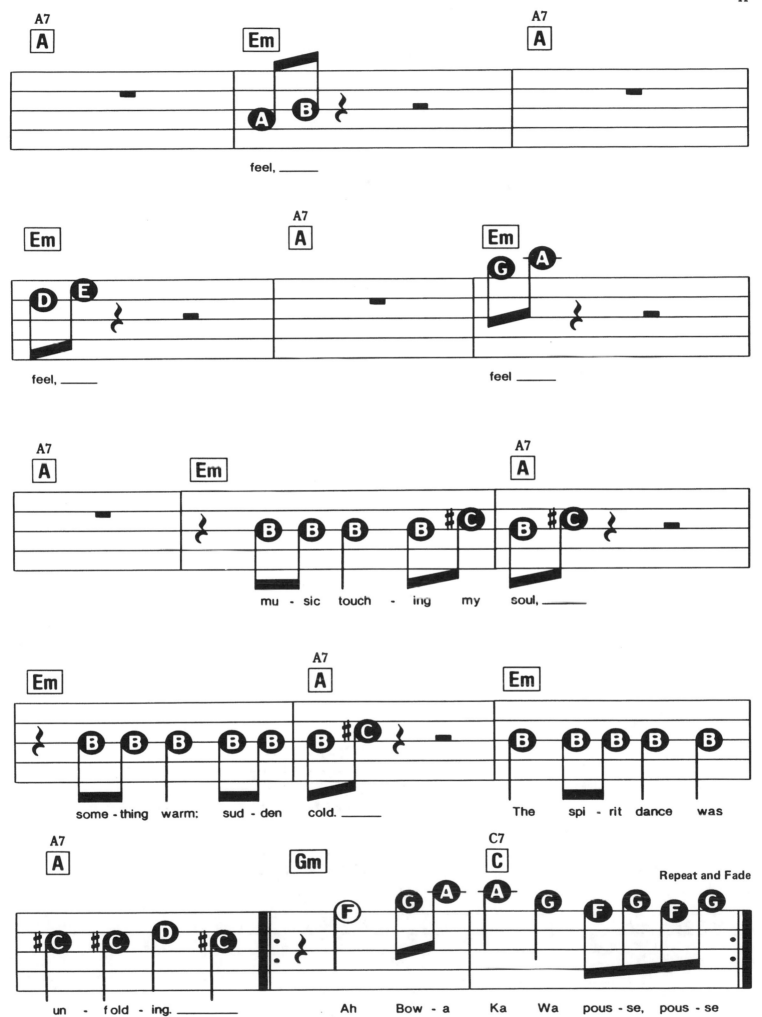

Mother

Registration 8
Rhythm: 8-Beat or Rock

Words and Music by
John Lennon

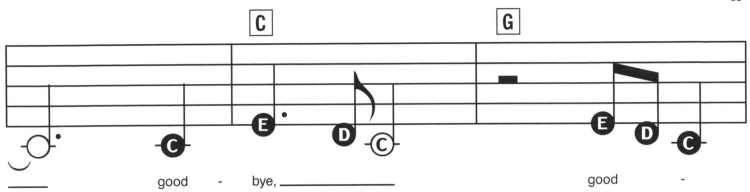

good - bye, _____ good -

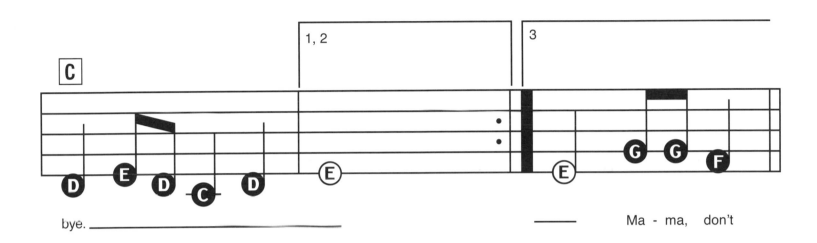

bye. _____ ___ Ma - ma, don't

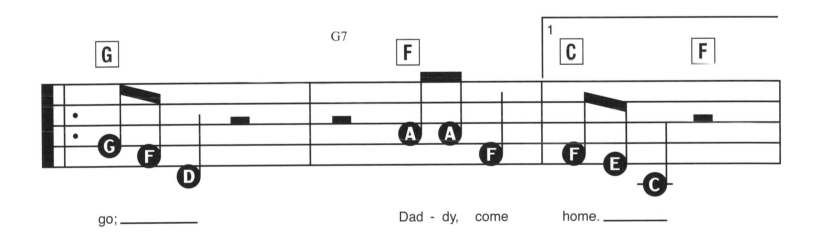

go; _____ Dad - dy, come home. _____

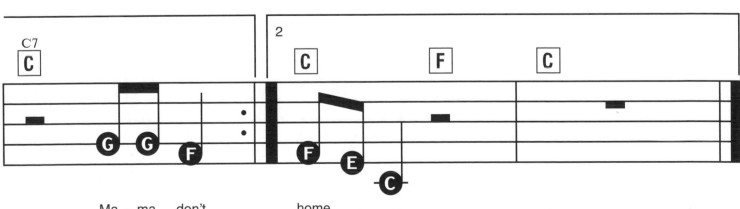

Ma - ma, don't home. _____

Nobody Told Me

Registration 4
Rhythm: Rock

Words and Music by
John Lennon

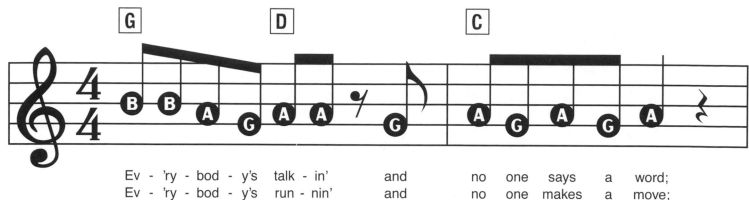

Ev - 'ry - bod - y's talk - in' and no one says a word;
Ev - 'ry - bod - y's run - nin' and no one makes a move;

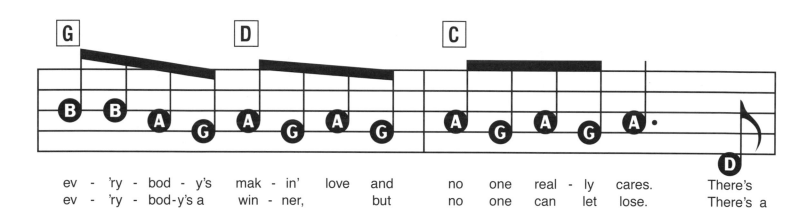

ev - 'ry - bod - y's mak - in' love and no one real - ly cares. There's
ev - 'ry - bod - y's a win - ner, but no one can let lose. There's a

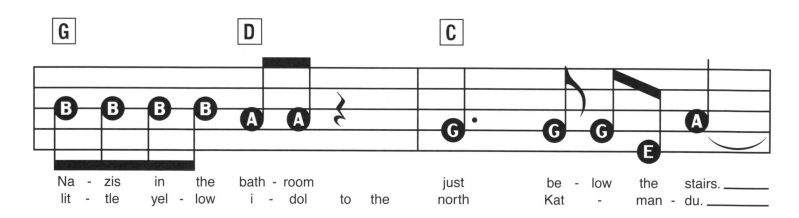

Na - zis in the bath - room just be - low the stairs. _____
lit - tle yel - low i - dol to the north Kat - man - du. _____

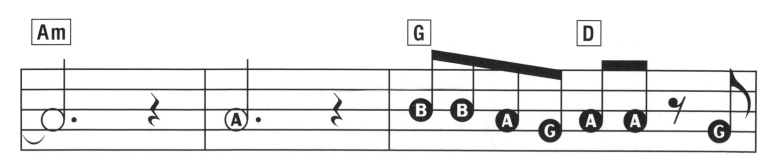

_____
_____
Al - ways some - thin' hap - penin' and
Ev - 'ry - bod - y's fly - in' and

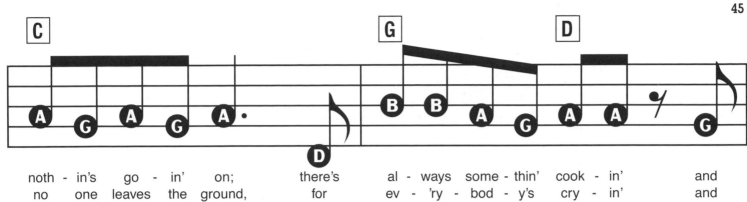

noth - in's go - in' on;   there's   al - ways some - thin' cook - in'   and
no one leaves the ground,   for   ev - 'ry - bod - y's cry - in'   and

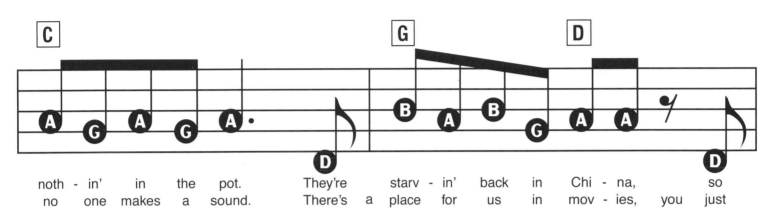

noth - in' in the pot.   They're starv - in' back in Chi - na,   so
no one makes a sound.   There's a place for us in mov - ies, you just

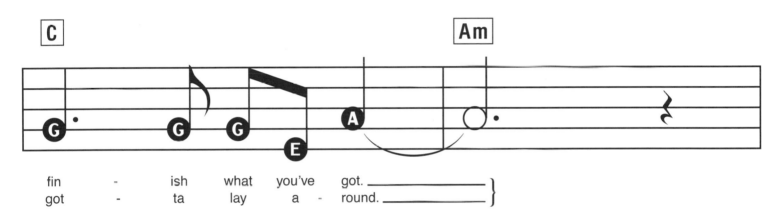

fin - ish what you've got. _____
got - ta lay a - round. _____

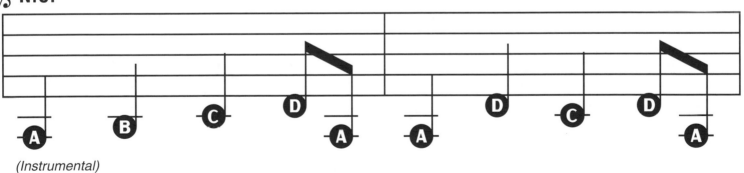

(Instrumental)

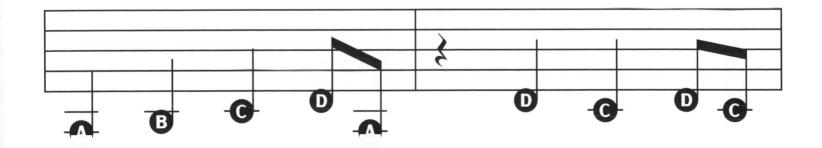

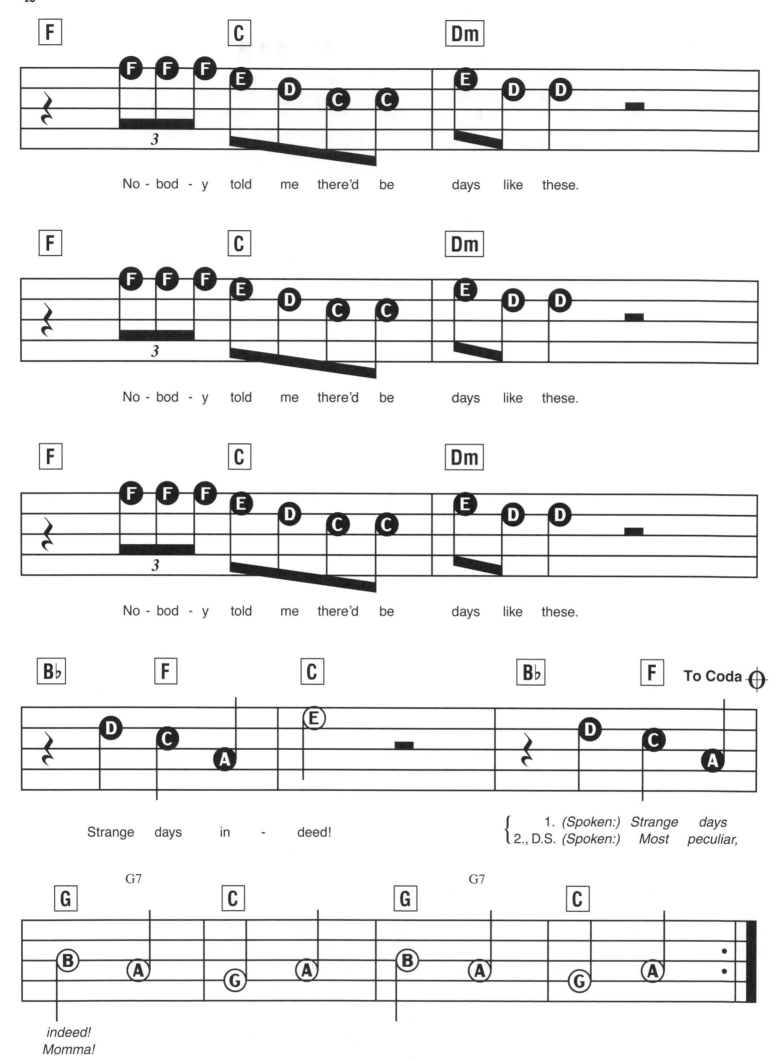

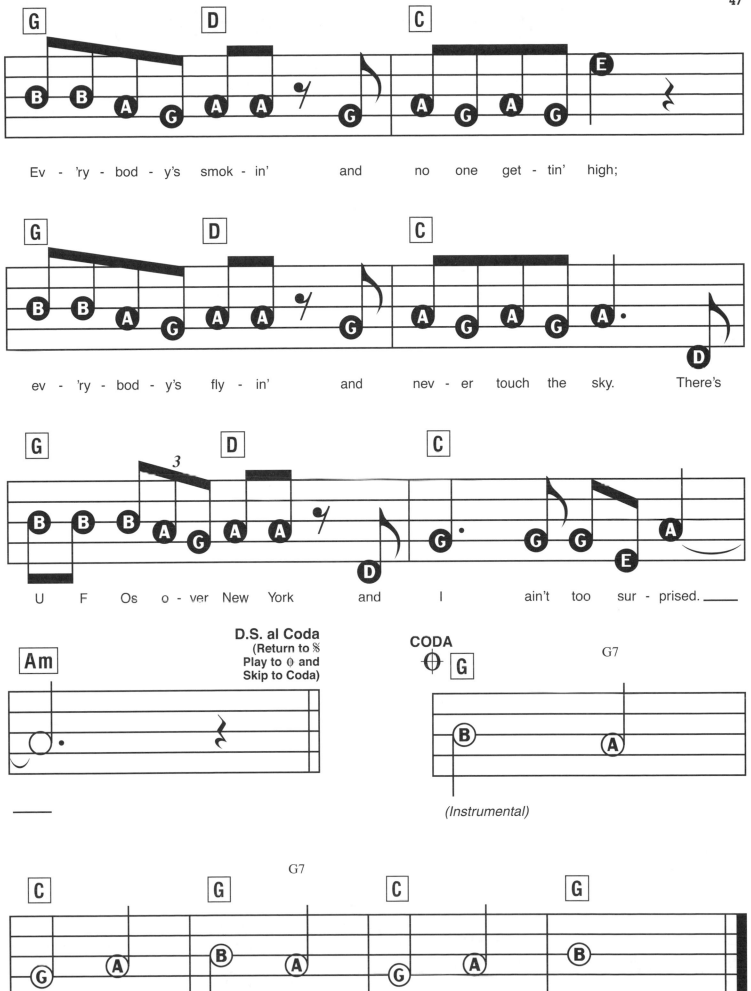

Ev - 'ry - bod - y's smok - in' and no one get - tin' high;

ev - 'ry - bod - y's fly - in' and nev - er touch the sky. There's

U F Os o - ver New York and I ain't too sur - prised. _____

D.S. al Coda
(Return to 𝄋
Play to ⊕ and
Skip to Coda)

CODA

(Instrumental)

Power to the People

Registration 5
Rhythm: Rock or Slow Rock

Words and Music by
John Lennon

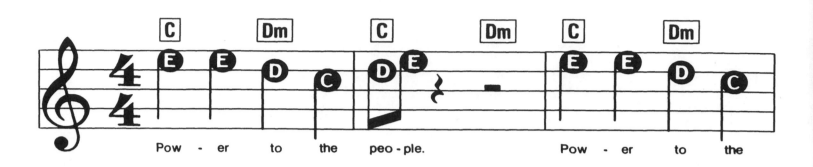

Pow - er   to the   peo - ple.   Pow - er   to the

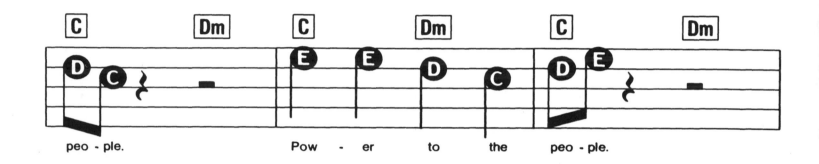

peo - ple.   Pow - er   to the   peo - ple.

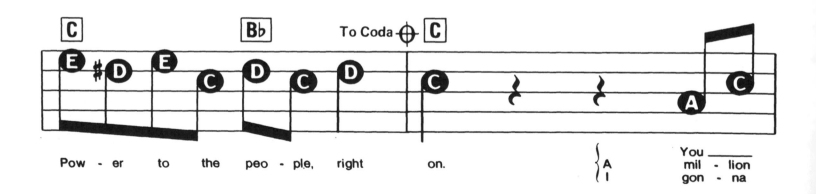

Pow - er   to the   peo - ple, right   on.   You ____
                                                                mil - lion
                                                                gon - na

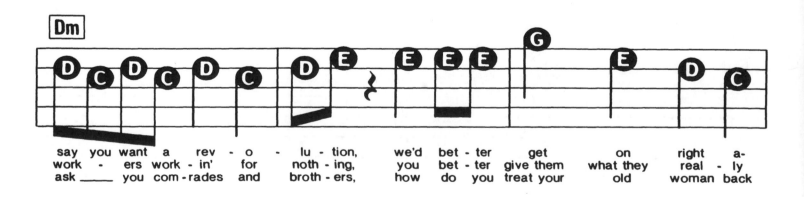

say you want a   rev - o - - lu - tion,   we'd bet - ter   get   on   right a-
work - ers work - in' for   noth - ing,   you bet - ter give them what they real - ly
ask ____ you com - rades and   broth - ers,   how do you treat your   old   woman back

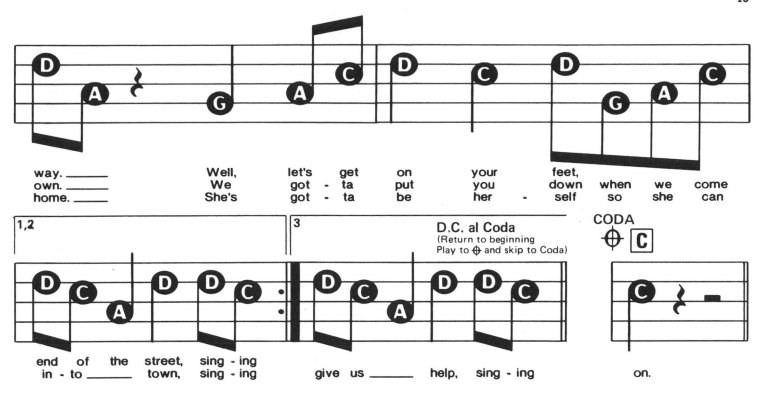

way. _____ Well,   let's get   on   your feet,
own. _____ We   got - ta put you   down when we come
home. _____ She's got - ta be her - self so she can

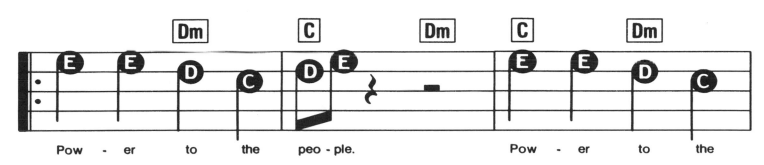

end of the street, sing - ing
in - to _____ town, sing - ing
          give us _____ help, sing - ing
on.

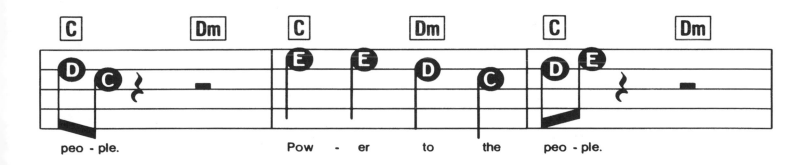

Pow - er   to   the   peo - ple.   Pow - er   to   the

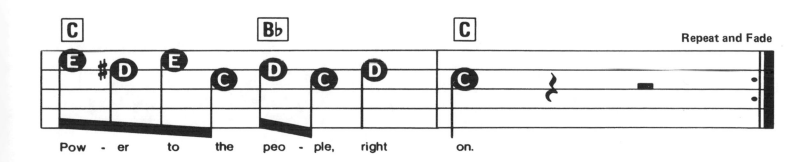

peo - ple.   Pow - er   to   the   peo - ple.

Pow - er   to   the   peo - ple, right   on.

Stand by Me

Registration 8
Rhythm: Country or Rock

Words and Music by Jerry Leiber,
Mike Stoller and Ben E. King

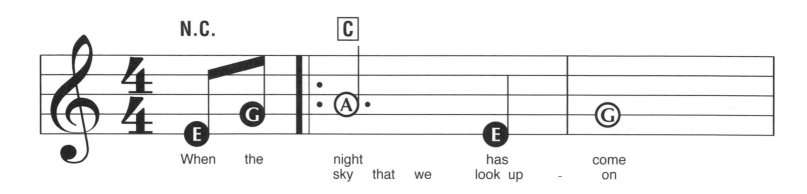

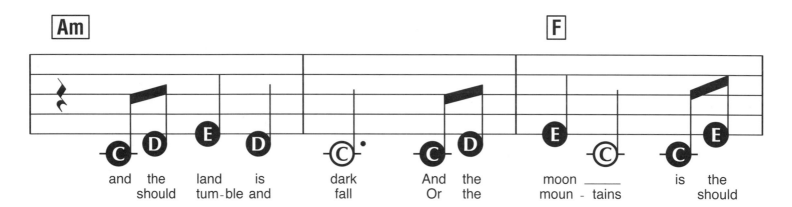

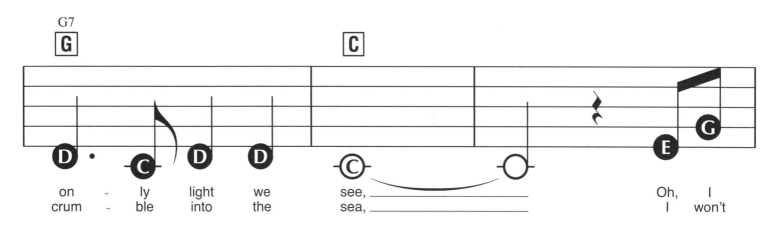

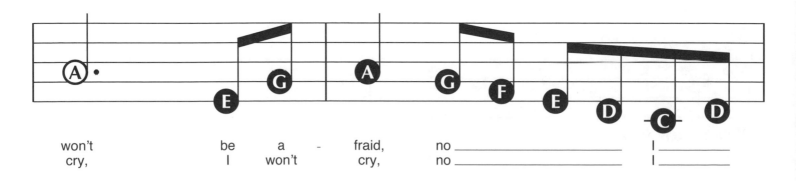

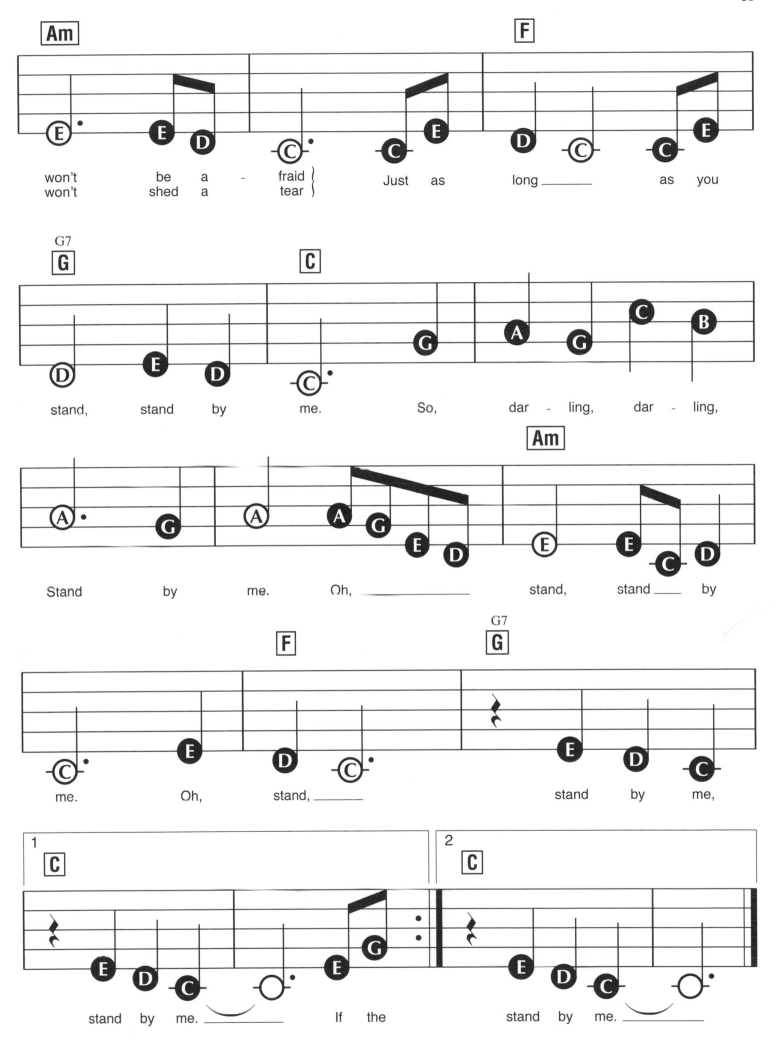

(Just Like) Starting Over

Registration 3
Rhythm: Slow Rock or Swing

Words and Music by
John Lennon

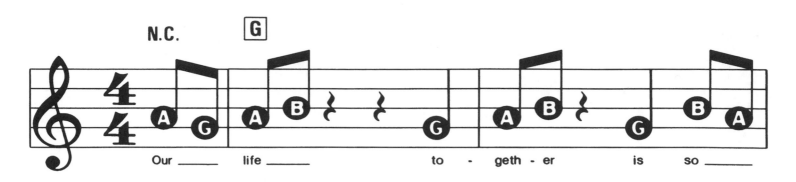

Our ____ life ____ to - geth - er is so ____

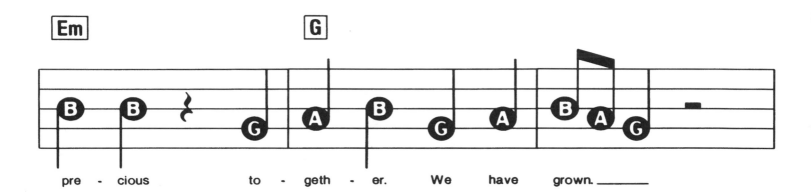

pre - cious to - geth - er. We have grown. ____

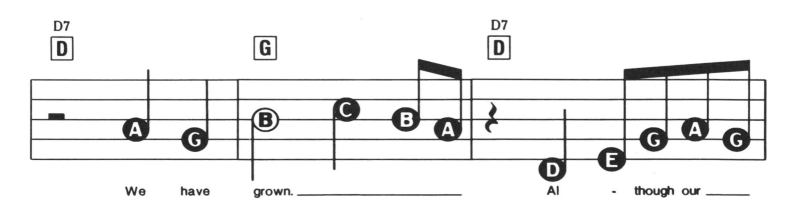

We have grown. _____ Al - though our ____

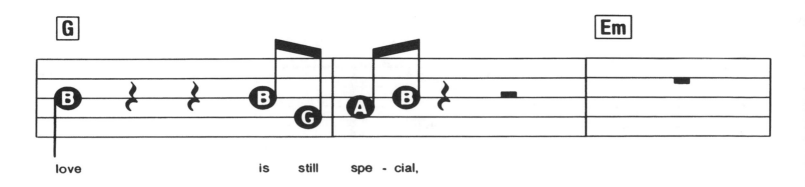

love is still spe - cial,

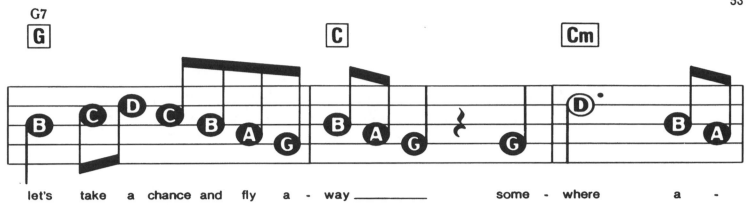

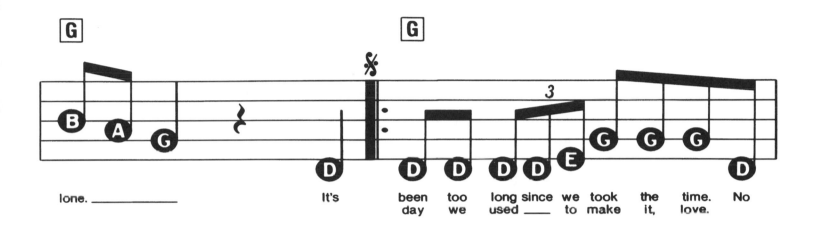

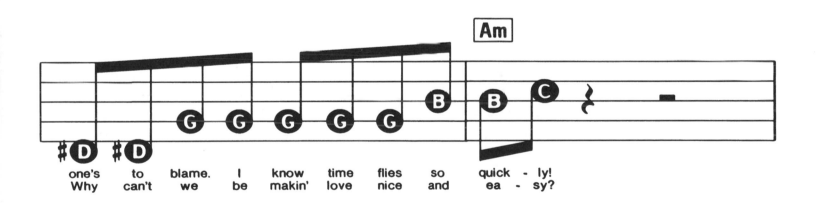

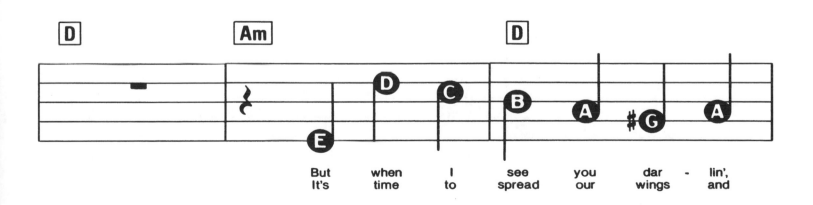

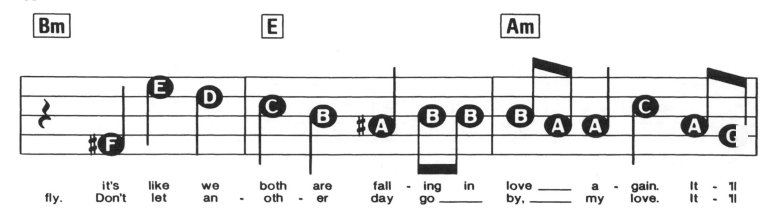

it's like we both are fall - ing in love _____ a - gain. It - 'll
fly. Don't let an - oth - er day go _____ by, _____ my love. It - 'll

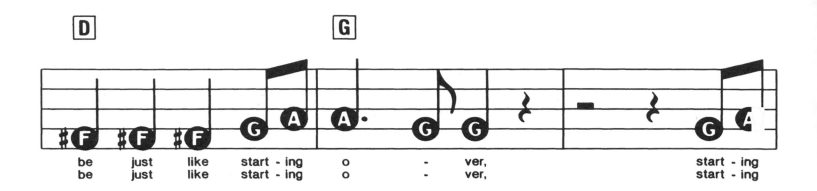

be just like start - ing o - ver, start - ing
be just like start - ing o - ver, start - ing

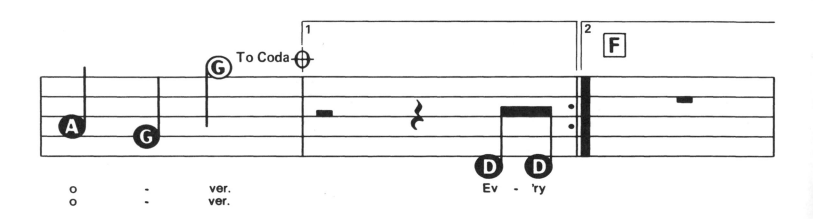

To Coda

o - ver. Ev - 'ry
o - ver.

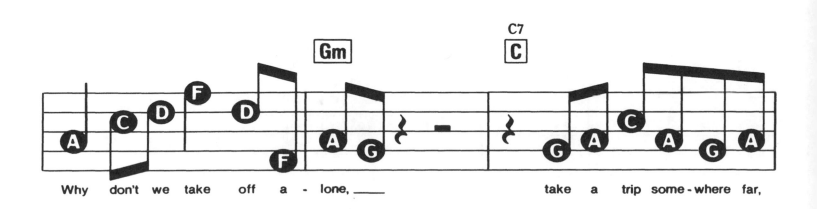

Why don't we take off a - lone, _____ take a trip some - where far,

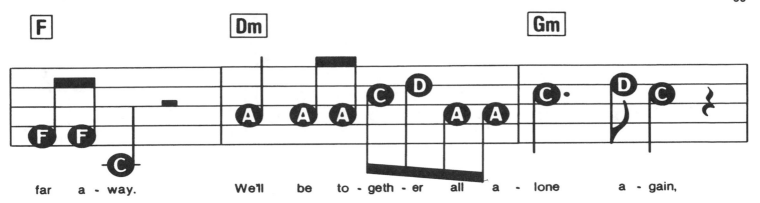

F   **Dm**   **Gm**

far a - way.   We'll be to - geth - er all a - lone a - gain,

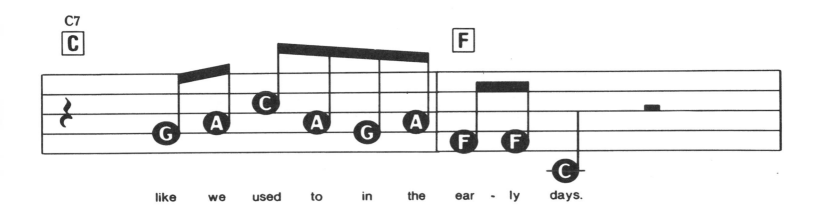

C7
C   **F**

like we used to in the ear - ly days.

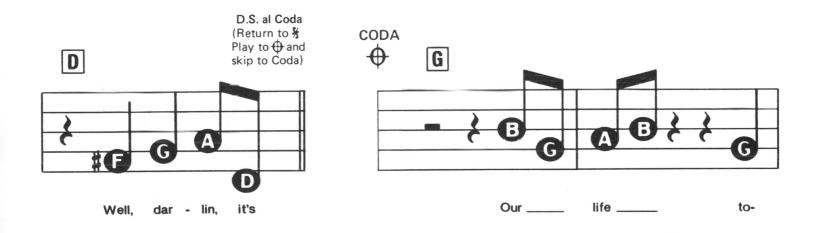

D

D.S. al Coda
(Return to 𝄋
Play to ⊕ and
skip to Coda)

CODA
⊕   **G**

Well, dar - lin, it's   Our ____ life ____ to-

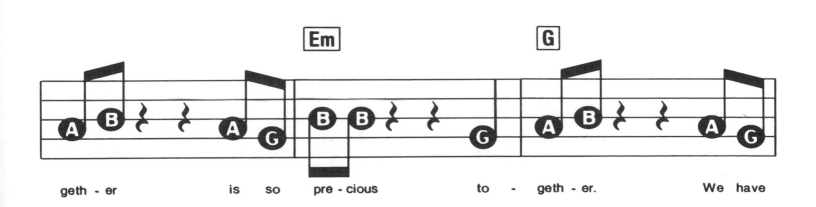

Em   **G**

geth - er   is so pre - cious to - geth - er. We have

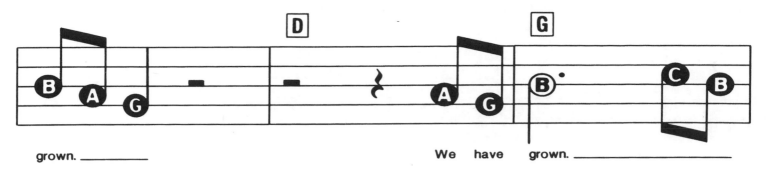

grown. _____

We have grown. _____

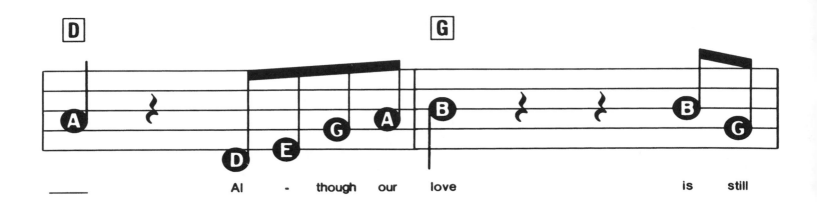

_____ Al - though our love is still

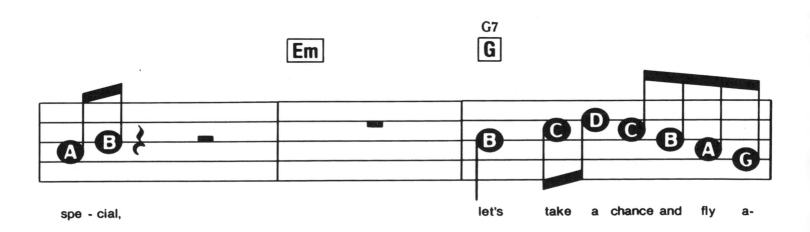

spe - cial, let's take a chance and fly a-

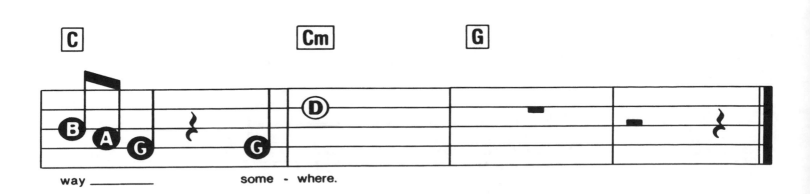

way _____ some - where.

Watching the Wheels

Registration 4
Rhythm: Rock or Jazz Rock

Words and Music by
John Lennon

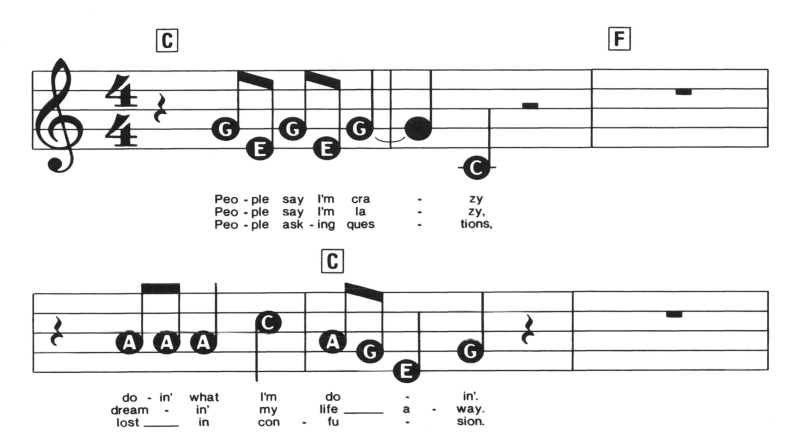

Peo - ple say I'm cra - zy
Peo - ple say I'm la - zy,
Peo - ple ask - ing ques - tions,

do - in' what I'm do - in'.
dream - in' my life ___ a - way.
lost ___ in con - fu - sion.

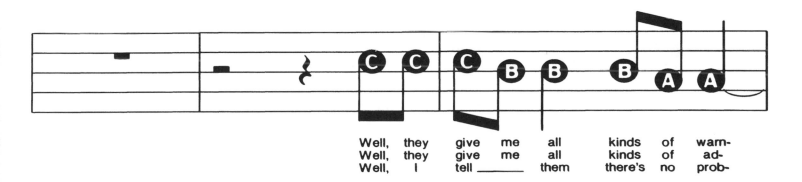

Well, they give me all kinds of warn-
Well, they give me all kinds of ad-
Well, I tell ___ them there's no prob-

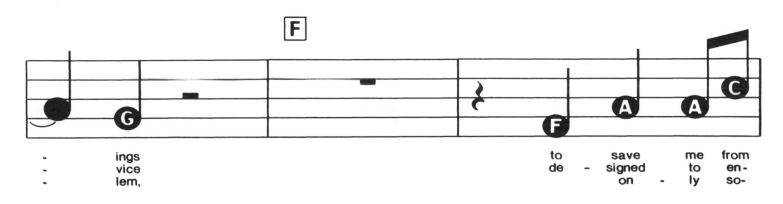

- ings
- vice
- lem,

to save me from
de - signed me to en-
on - ly so-

58

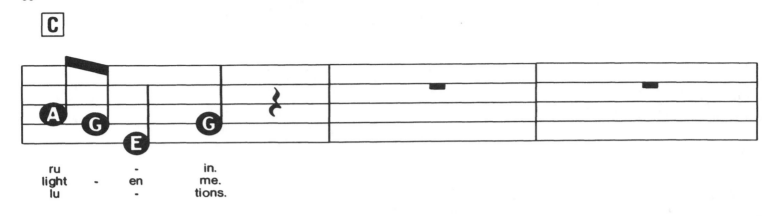

ru - in.
light - en me.
lu - tions.

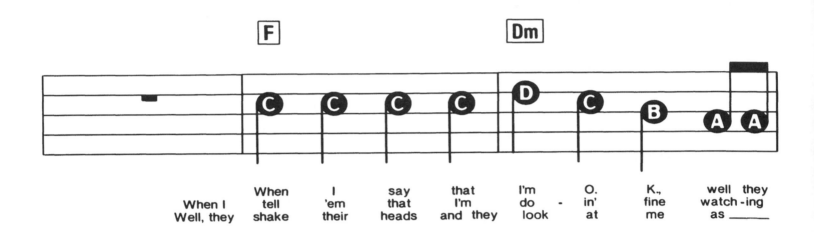

When I When I say that I'm O. K., well they
Well, they tell 'em that I'm do - in' fine watch -ing
shake their heads and they look at me as _____

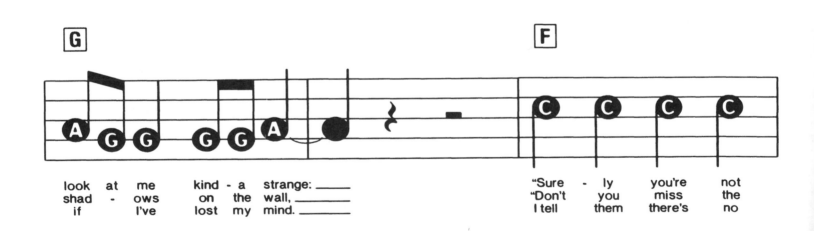

look at me kind - a strange: _____
shad - ows on the wall, _____
if I've lost my mind. _____

"Sure - ly you're not
"Don't you miss the
I tell them there's no

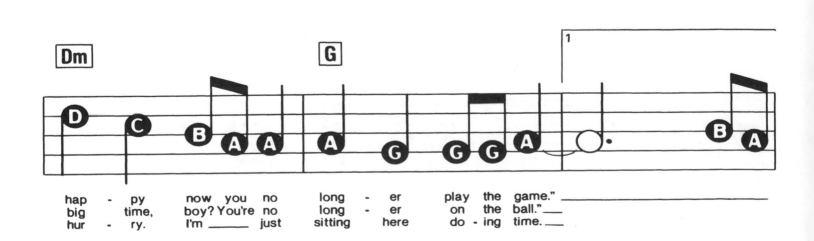

hap - py now you no long - er play the game." _____
big time, boy? You're no long - er on the ball."_____
hur - ry. I'm _____ just sitting here do - ing time. _____

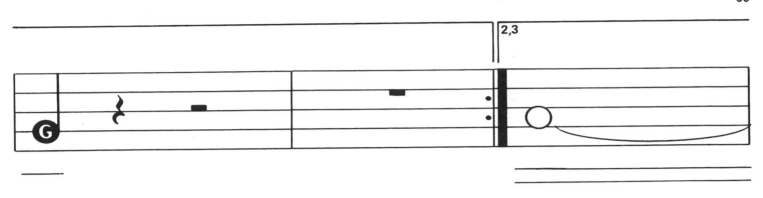

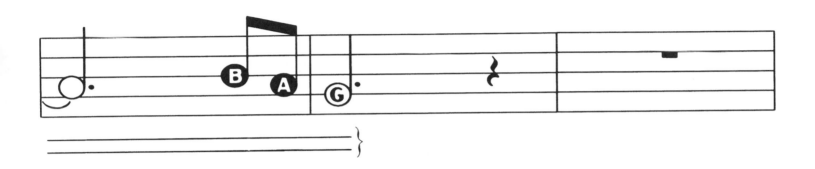

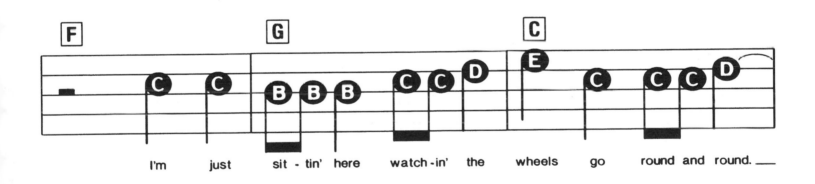

I'm just sit-tin' here watch-in' the wheels go round and round. ___

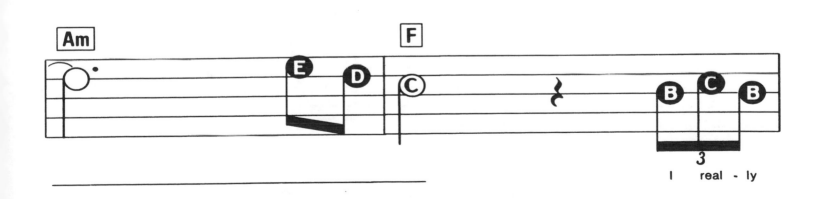

I real - ly

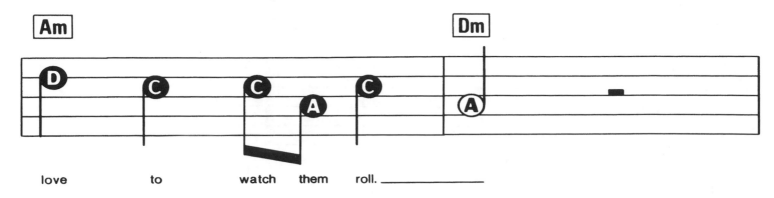

love   to   watch   them   roll. _____

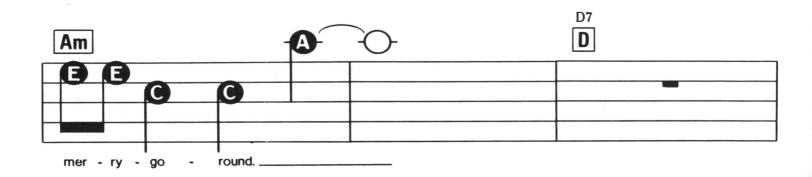

No   long - er   rid - ing   on   the

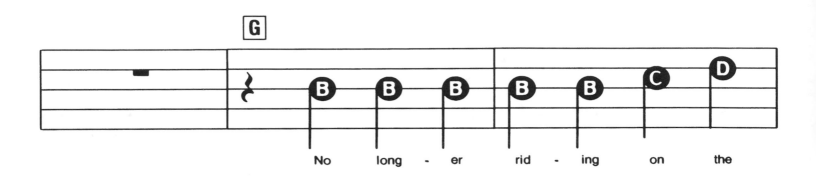

mer - ry - go - round. _____

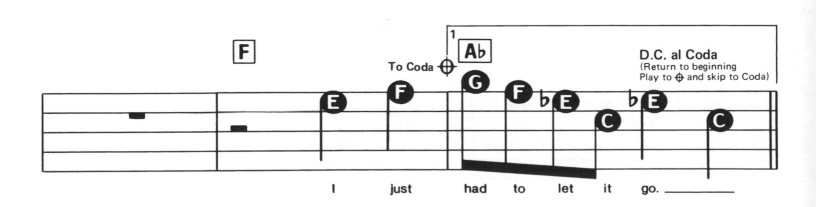

I   just   had   to   let   it   go. _____

To Coda

D.C. al Coda
(Return to beginning
Play to ⊕ and skip to Coda)

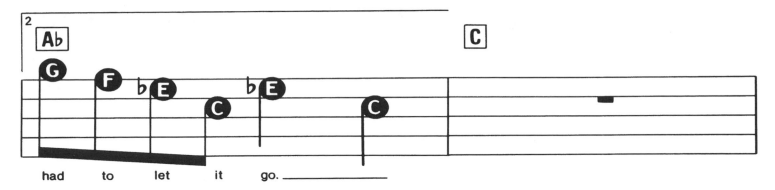

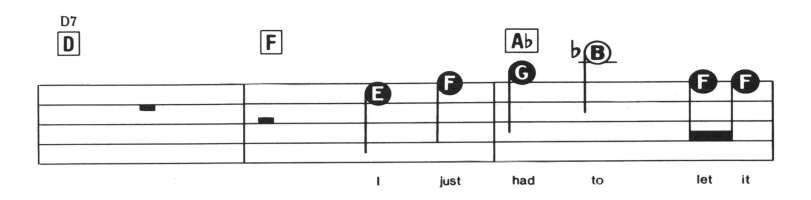

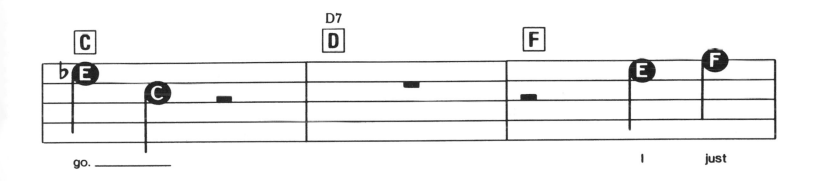

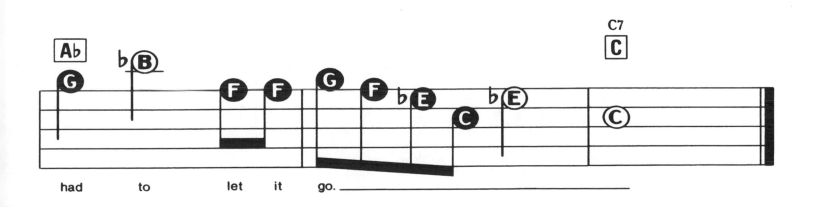

Whatever Gets You Through the Night

Registration 4
Rhythm: Slow Rock or Swing

Words and Music by
John Lennon

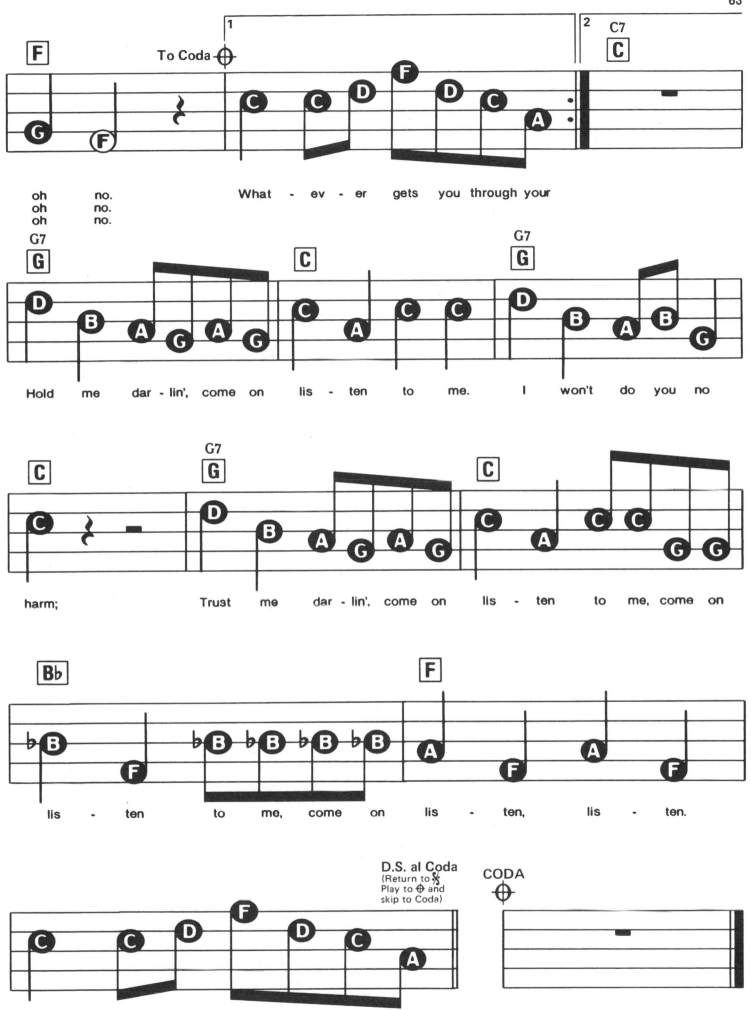

Working Class Hero

Registration 2
Rhythm: Waltz

Words and Music by
John Lennon

N.C. | Am | G

E | E E E | E D C | D C D

1. As soon as you're born, _____ they make you feel
2. hurt you at home and they hit you at
3. tor - tured and scared you for twen - ty odd
4.-5. *(See additional lyrics)*

Am

E | (E) | | E

small _____
school. _____
years, _____

by
They

C C C | C B | A | G B A G B A

giv - ing you no time in - stead of it all. _____
hate you if you're clev - er in and they de - spise a fool. _____
then they ex - pect you to pick a ca - reer. _____

Am

A | (A) | | E E

_____
_____
_____

Till the
Till you're
When you

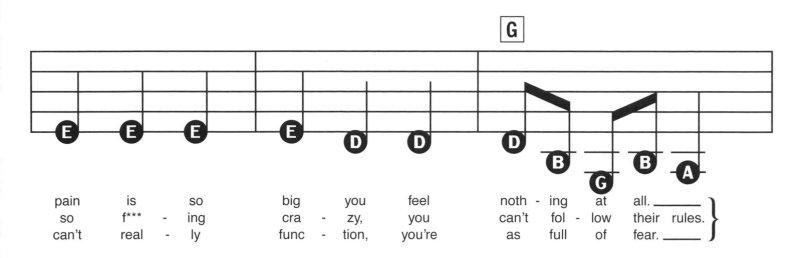

pain | is | so | big | you | feel | noth - ing | at | all. _____
so | f*** - | ing | cra - | zy, | you | can't | fol - low | their rules.
can't | real - | ly | func - | tion, | you're | as | full of | fear. _____

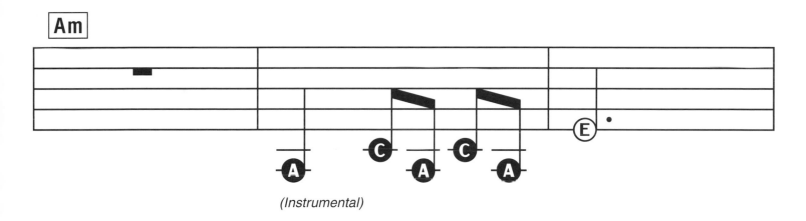

(Instrumental)

Chorus

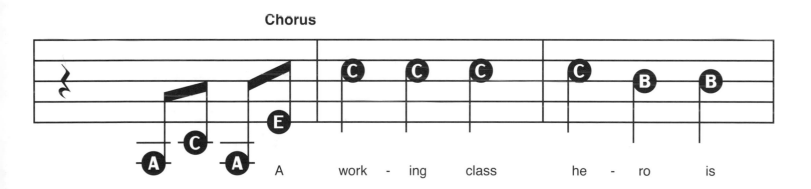

A work - ing class he - ro is

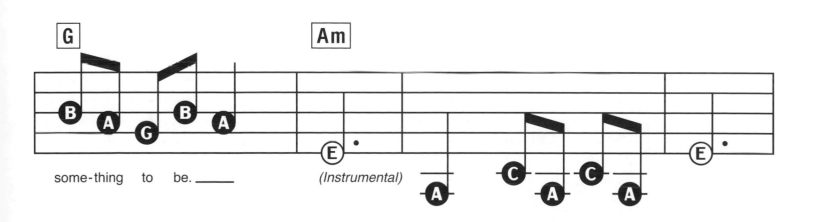

some-thing to be. _____ *(Instrumental)*

66

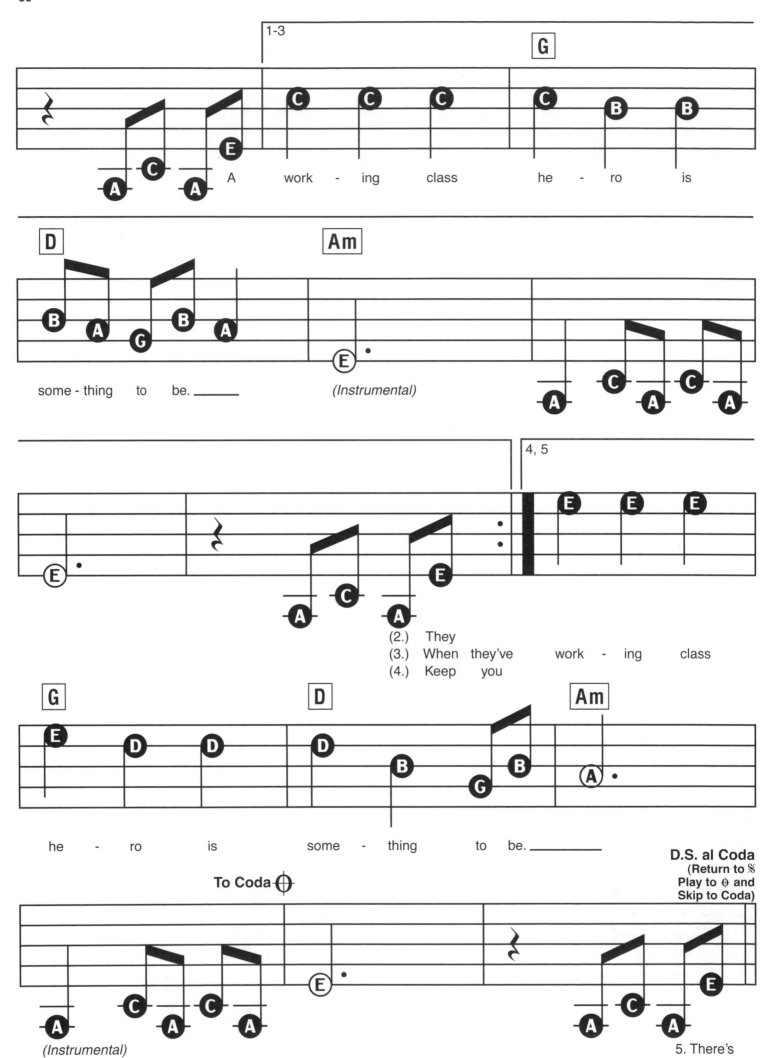

CODA

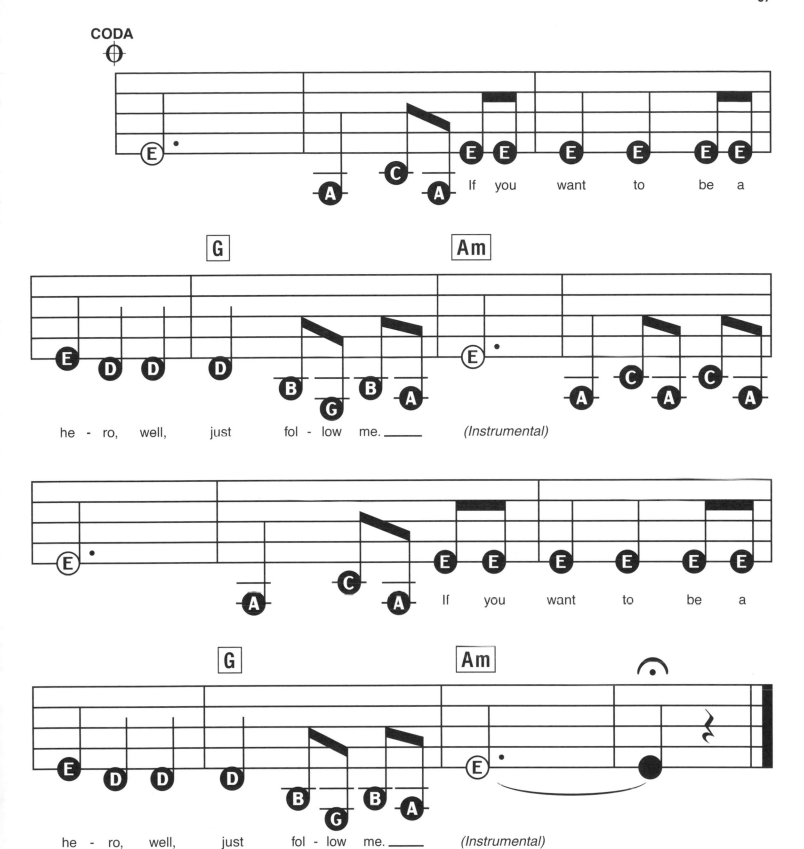

he - ro, well, just fol - low me.＿ (Instrumental)

he - ro, well, just fol - low me.＿ (Instrumental)

Additional Lyrics

4. Keep you doped with religion and sex and TV,
   And you think you're so clever and classless and free,
   But you're still f***ing peasants as far as I can see.
   Chorus

5. There's room at the top they are telling you still,
   But first you must learn how to smile as you kill
   If you want to be like the folks on the hill.
   Chorus

Woman

Registration 3
Rhythm: Rock or Jazz Rock

Words and Music by
John Lennon

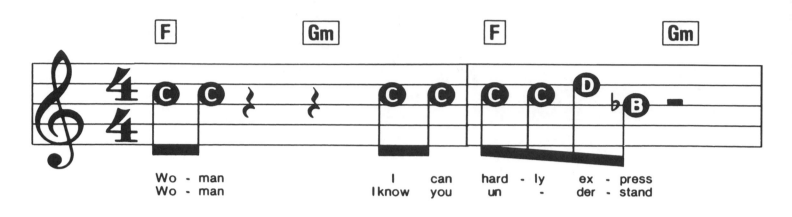

Wo - man   I   can   hard - ly   ex - press
Wo - man   I know   you   un -   der - stand

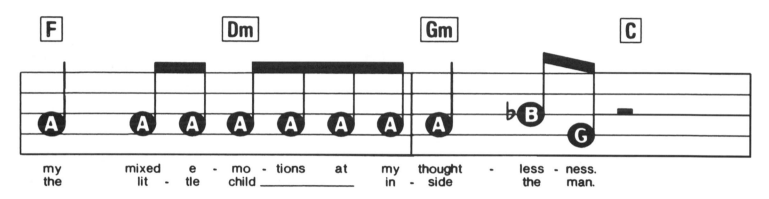

my   mixed   e - mo - tions   at   my   thought - less - ness.
the   lit - tle   child _____   in - side   the   man.

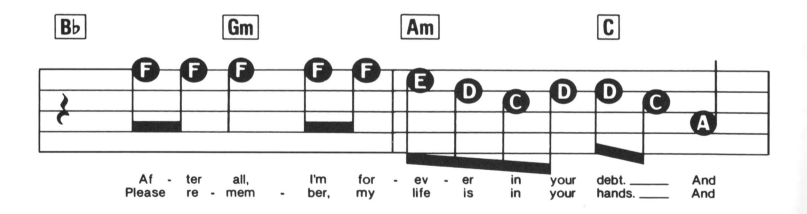

Af - ter   all,   I'm   for - ev - er   in   your   debt. ____   And
Please   re - mem - ber,   my   life   is   in   your   hands. ____   And

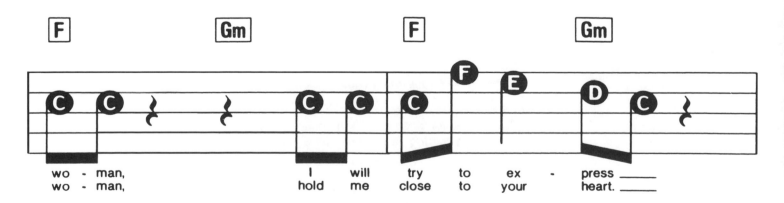

wo - man,   I   will   try   to   ex - press ____
wo - man,   hold   me   close   to   your   heart. ____

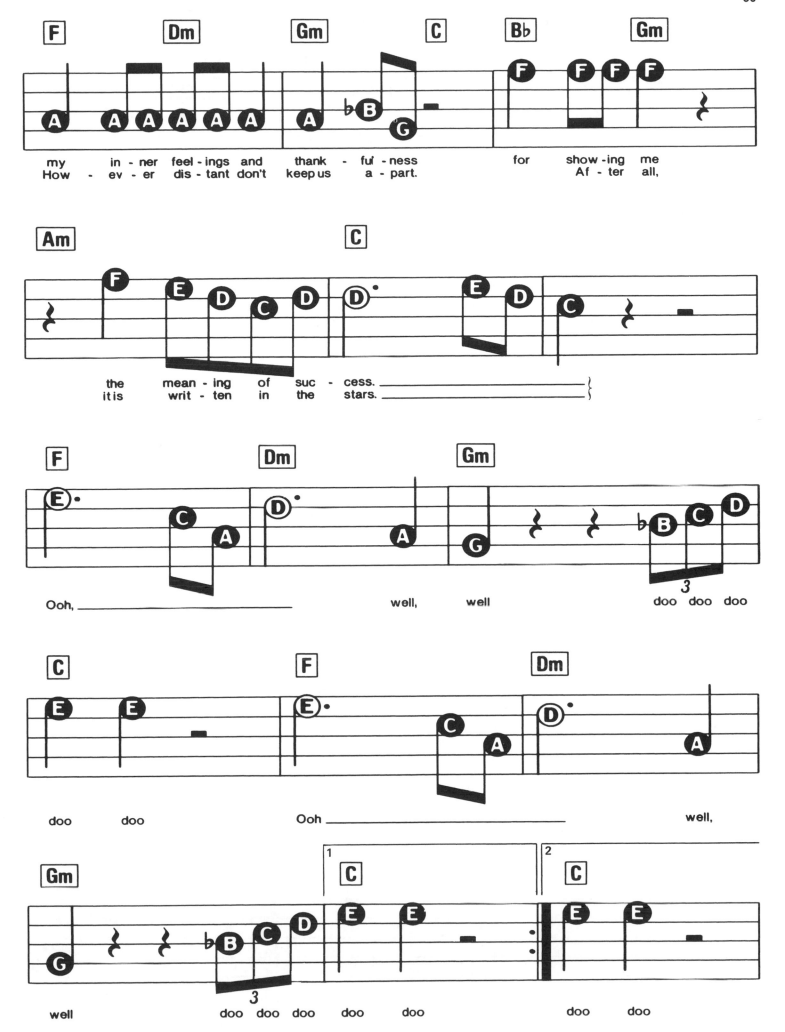

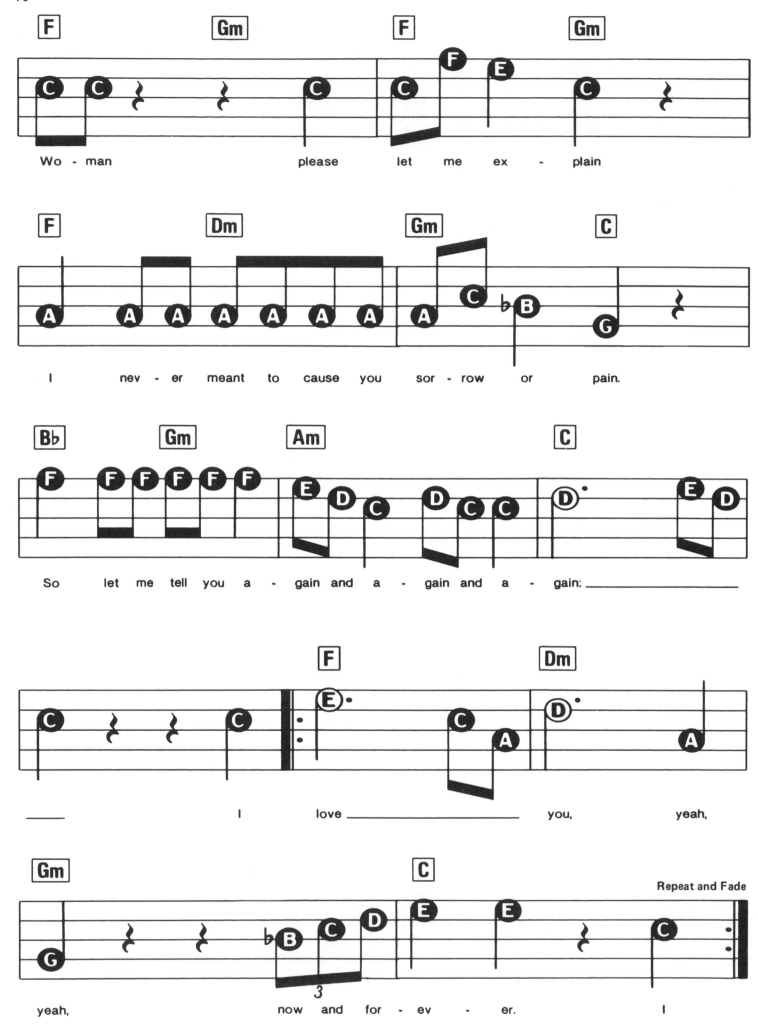

Registration Guide

- Match the Registration number on the song to the corresponding numbered category below. Select and activate an instrumental sound available on your instrument.

- Choose an automatic rhythm appropriate to the mood and style of the song. (Consult your Owner's Guide for proper operation of automatic rhythm features.)

- Adjust the tempo and volume controls to comfortable settings.

Registration

1	Mellow	Flutes, Clarinet, Oboe, Flugel Horn, Trombone, French Horn, Organ Flutes
2	Ensemble	Brass Section, Sax Section, Wind Ensemble, Full Organ, Theater Organ
3	Strings	Violin, Viola, Cello, Fiddle, String Ensemble, Pizzicato, Organ Strings
4	Guitars	Acoustic/Electric Guitars, Banjo, Mandolin, Dulcimer, Ukulele, Hawaiian Guitar
5	Mallets	Vibraphone, Marimba, Xylophone, Steel Drums, Bells, Celesta, Chimes
6	Liturgical	Pipe Organ, Hand Bells, Vocal Ensemble, Choir, Organ Flutes
7	Bright	Saxophones, Trumpet, Mute Trumpet, Synth Leads, Jazz/Gospel Organs
8	Piano	Piano, Electric Piano, Honky Tonk Piano, Harpsichord, Clavi
9	Novelty	Melodic Percussion, Wah Trumpet, Synth, Whistle, Kazoo, Perc. Organ
10	Bellows	Accordion, French Accordion, Mussette, Harmonica, Pump Organ, Bagpipes